Introducing Delphi ORM

ORM

Object Relational Mapping Using TMS Aurelius

John Kouraklis

Apress®

Introducing Delphi ORM: Object Relational Mapping Using TMS Aurelius

John Kouraklis
London, UK

ISBN-13 (pbk): 978-1-4842-5012-9   ISBN-13 (electronic): 978-1-4842-5013-6
https://doi.org/10.1007/978-1-4842-5013-6

Managing Director, Apress Media LLC: Welmoed Spahr
Acquisitions Editor: Steve Anglin
Development Editor: Matthew Moodie
Coordinating Editor: Mark Powers

Cover designed by eStudioCalamar

Cover image designed by Freepik (www.freepik.com)

Distributed to the book trade worldwide by Springer Science+Business Media New York, 233 Spring Street, 6th Floor, New York, NY 10013. Phone 1-800-SPRINGER, fax (201) 348-4505, e-mail orders-ny@springer-sbm.com, or visit www.springeronline.com. Apress Media, LLC is a California LLC and the sole member (owner) is Springer Science + Business Media Finance Inc (SSBM Finance Inc). SSBM Finance Inc is a **Delaware** corporation.

For information on translations, please e-mail editorial@apress.com; for reprint, paperback, or audio rights, please email bookpermissions@springernature.com.

Apress titles may be purchased in bulk for academic, corporate, or promotional use. eBook versions and licenses are also available for most titles. For more information, reference our Print and eBook Bulk Sales web page at http://www.apress.com/bulk-sales.

Any source code or other supplementary material referenced by the author in this book is available to readers on GitHub via the book's product page, located at www.apress.com/9781484250129. For more detailed information, please visit http://www.apress.com/source-code.

Printed on acid-free paper

To my dream Anna

Table of Contents

About the Author

John Kouraklis started exploring computers when he was 16 and since then has followed all the way from Turbo Pascal to the latest Delphi versions as a hobby initially and as a profession for most of his adult life. He has developed a wide range of applications, from financial software to reverse engineering tools, including an application for professional gamblers. He is also the author of *MVVM in Delphi* (Apress, 2016).

About the Technical Reviewers

Wagner Landgraf holds a Bachelor of Science in Electronic Engineering and a Master of Science in Industrial Computing.

He has 24 years of experience with Delphi development and is the Manager of TMS Business product line at TMS Software, where he serves as Architect and core developer of products such as TMS Aurelius and TMS XData.

Nick Hodges is a Software Development Manager at Gateway Ticketing Systems, a firm that provides ticketing and access control systems to the largest amusement parks, zoos, and museums around the world. Nick is a software developer at heart. He's been a Pascal/Delphi developer for over 20 years and still thinks that Delphi is the best development tool out there. He loves to read programming books, attend conferences, and watch cool videos about new programming techniques. He generally tries to be an industry thought leader.

Introduction

Modern software development techniques rely almost exclusively on object-oriented programming (OOP). This approach promotes a specific paradigm that sees fundamental design units (objects) as containers that encapsulate both data and logic (code) and, in many instances, indicates how specific data that stem from business logic should be mapped. This convoluted view contradicts with the other important pillar of information age: the databases.

Storing data and managing databases take developers to a world with different design principles and concepts. Table design, SQL query optimization, and joined table operations are only a few notions that indicate the existence and requirement of different skill sets. On top of this, if one considers the abundance of database engines available in the market and the technical specificity of each one of them, it is not hard to realize the challenges software developers may face given the fact that modern applications rely on the ability to store data in a persistent medium.

Object relational mapping (ORM) frameworks attempt to bring the two worlds of OOP and databases together and provide a toolbox which abstracts the specific requirements of each database. As a result, developers are free to focus on ways to raise business value of their software solutions rather than consuming resources in understanding how to make databases work. ORM promotes reusable coding, automation and standardization of data-related processes, separation of concerns as data access and layers are isolated, and abstraction of database engines; this means that coders who employ ORM libraries are free to switch between databases or even employ different databases without changing a single line of code.

TMS Aurelius is an ORM library developed by TMS Software and targets the Delphi development environment. It is a modern, robust, and efficient approach to the use of databases in an OOP fashion.

This book is dedicated to Aurelius and the Delphi developers who want to make the most out of the framework. It offers a guide in how to embed Aurelius in Delphi projects and how to implement basic and advanced queries, and it moves forward by showing how Aurelius can be used in mobile platforms and in cooperation with third-party providers of JSON-based data.

Who This Book Is For

This book is the perfect companion to both newcomers to Aurelius and to more experienced developers with the framework. It assumes some knowledge of Delphi as it requires familiarity with the IDE and the features of the language. Nevertheless, Aurelius is also available for Lazarus and, therefore, this book appeals to Pascal developers who favor that environment as well.

After reading this book, you will be able to

- Appreciate the different workflows related to the use of databases as seen from the coder's side

- Assess the different uses and features of TMS Aurelius

- Design applications which use TMS Aurelius

The Development Environment

The code presented in this book is developed using the following environment:

- Embarcadero Delphi 10 Rio Professional

- Microsoft Windows 10 Professional

- FireMonkey framework

- TMS Aurelius 4.4

- Android Nougat

- Steema TeeChart v2018 Standard Evaluation Version

I use the Professional version of Delphi, but I do not use any features exclusive to this version. You can use whichever edition you have access to. I also prefer to develop multi-device applications but this is not a requirement; you can very easily use Aurelius in VCL applications as well. The only exception to this is the projects that show how Aurelius can be used in mobile platforms; these projects require FireMonkey.

Lastly, in Chapter 7, where Aurelius consumes data from remote servers, I use TMS XData 4.5 Trial version and in Chapter 8 TMS Data Modeler 3.3 is required.

The Book's Structure

This book has eight chapters. It starts with basic theoretical concepts, then proceeds to the introduction of TMS Aurelius, and as chapters develop it gradually explores different features of the framework.

Chapter 1: In the Land of ORM

This chapter visits fundamental concepts of ORM frameworks and explores different workflows related to them. It also provides a short discussion of ORM terminology.

Chapter 2: TMS Aurelius

This chapter introduces TMS Aurelius. It starts by discussing different versions and installation options of the product and shows how the fundamental ideas in ORM that are presented in Chapter 1 are implemented by the framework. This is the first exposure of the reader to code related to Aurelius.

Chapter 3: Call Center Application

This chapter introduces the CallCentre application. This is an application that presents data from a call center and organizes it in different ways (by department, by agent, etc.). The data set provides some great opportunities to show how Aurelius features work.

Chapter 4: Basic Operations

In this chapter, we start with basic operations such as how to add, update, and remove entries from the database. We, also, deal with managing nullable and blob fields, and we see how Aurelius can execute large number of SQL statements.

Chapter 5: Querying the Database

The topic of this chapter is how to build and expand on more sophisticated queries that allow manipulation of data at database level. OOP would indicate that calculations and grouping of data occur in code, whereas database programming relies on the underlying database engine. In this chapter, we see how Aurelius can bring the two together.

Chapter 6: Enhancements

This chapter looks at more advanced concepts in Aurelius (events, inheritance) and visits the TAureliusDataSet.

Chapter 7: Aurelius on the Move

As mobile platforms and the Internet become essential part of application development, this chapter takes the task to move Aurelius to mobile platforms. The chapter shows what changes are required for this task and explores different options in this direction.

Chapter 8: TMS Data Modeler

TMS Data Modeler is a stand-alone application by TMS Software that assists Aurelius users in many ways. This chapter explores the different features of the application and shows how it can contribute to productivity and efficiency.

Code Files

This book comes with Delphi code files. You can access the code by clicking the **Download Source Code** button located at www.apress. com/9781484250129. Table 1 provides a summary of the project names used in the book along with some notes.

Table 1. *Project Names Per Chapter*

Chapter	Folder\Project Name	Notes
	Misc	This folder contains miscellaneous files that are used in different chapters (image files, data sets, SQL scripts, etc.)
2	Chapter 2\BasicFeatures	Demonstrates very basic features in a console application
3	Chapter 3\CallCentre (Skeleton)	Provides a project that shows the GUI of the example application. All the subsequent projects are based on this one

(continued)

Table 1. (*continued*)

Chapter	Folder\Project Name	Notes
	Chapter 3\CallCentre (Without Database Session)	Demonstrates the use of entities, connections, and database manager
	Chapter 3\CallCentre (With Database Session)	Replaces TDatabaseManager with IDatabase Session
4	Chapter 4\CallCentre (Without Utilities)	Adds the ability to provide basic operations to entities
	Chapter 4\CallCentre (With Utilities)	Adds basic utilities to handle blobs and exceptions
	Chapter 4\CallCentre (Import)	Demonstrates how to set the object manager in transactional state
5	Chapter 5\CallCentre (Listings)	Shows the call lists for agents and departments
	Chapter 5\CallCentre (Queries)	Adds key calculations based on queries
	Chapter 5\CallCentre (Views)	Demonstrates the use of views
6	Chapter 6\CallCentre (Inheritance)	Demonstrates different inheritance strategies in Aurelius
	Chapter 6\CallCentre (Events)	Demonstrates the use of events
	Chapter 6\CallCentre (TAureliusDataSet)	Demonstrates different ways to populate TAureliusDataSet

(*continued*)

Table 1. (*continued*)

Chapter	Folder\Project Name	Notes
7	Chapter 7\CallCentre (Local)	Adapted project to run on Android
	Chapter 7\User	A simple project to fetch JSON content from third-party providers
	Chapter 7\Client	Shows how to use Aurelius to consume data based on REST API from third-parties
	Chapter 7\XData	Demonstrates the use of Aurelius and XData server
8	Chapter 8\CallCentre.dgp	Data Modeler project

CHAPTER 1

In the Land of ORM

Object relational mapping (ORM) represents a set of techniques in computer programming, which attempt to make incompatible systems cooperate, communicate, and exchange information. At the same time, they attempt to make the life of developers easier.

The systems in discussion are database systems and systems that evolve from the dominant paradigm of object-oriented programming (OOP). Databases are designed to store and provide access to various data types in a persistent way. Data is stored in databases and outlives the execution of the applications that use it. On the other hand, developers that follow OOP principles think in a very different way when it comes to the representation of data in their applications.

The design of database systems has advanced considerably over the decades, and today databases represent both reliable and stable systems which are found in almost every type of applications. The widespread use of Internet, the domination of social media, and the ability to generate high volume of data in real time and in high velocity (big data) have led to a wide range of database systems with various degrees of sophistication and implementation complexity. As a result, database administrators enjoy a wealth of options – databases that follow the traditional relationship-based design (RDBMS/SQL) to systems without inherent structure like the NoSQL database.

The design of relational database systems has served the information world extremely well since their invention. Looking at the heart of relational database management systems (RDBMS), one can observe

© John Kouraklis 2019

J. Kouraklis, *Introducing Delphi ORM*, https://doi.org/10.1007/978-1-4842-5013-6_1

though that the fundamental elements have not changed drastically in terms of the way data is stored and considered. One of the most persistent designs of databases is the type of data those systems are capable of storing. Put simply, the vast majority of databases can manage data of simple types (scalar). Data types like integers, chars, strings, bytes, and dates are in their natural environment with databases.

On the other hand, developers in OOP see the world with the eyes of nonscalar concepts as they are represented by objects. Objects have attributes and properties (object-based design) but also provide mechanisms to manipulate the behavior of objects via the concepts of polymorphism and inheritance (object-oriented design). Polymorphism allows developers to change the behavior of an object or a function depending on the associated elements, and inheritance creates a form of hierarchy between objects allowing common attributes and behavior. Objects, although a common feature in modern programming languages, are quite complex in terms of implementation and are not compatible with the way databases manage data. Additionally, more complex structures like lists, maps, and dictionaries found in programming languages and used every day by developers cannot be mapped easily to the storage mechanism of databases (Mueller, 2013).

Communication Between Incompatible Systems

Consider the example of a blog site. Users register and create posts. Posts can have a number of tags or categories. From the database designer's point of view, users can be represented by the table Users, posts by the table Posts, and tags and categories by the tables Tags and Categories, respectively. Concepts like "*a user owns several posts*" and "*posts have many categories*" are implemented by different types of relationships (one-to-one, one-to-many, many-to-many). Figure 1-1 shows a simplified database model for the blog site.

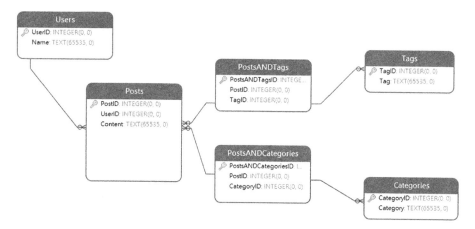

Figure 1-1. *Simplified database model for a blog site*

This representation is only a conceptual model. At database level, database designers and administrators see the preceding model in terms of records (rows in a table) and columns (fields of a table). A more accurate representation would be Figure 1-2 where real content is being stored in a database and presented in the form of records (rows). The relationships that Figure 1-1 indicates are not visible at this level as they are forced by the database engine. Moreover, one can observe the simple data types the records hold. Although this is a simplified example, the values and, therefore, their data types are representative of more complex situations.

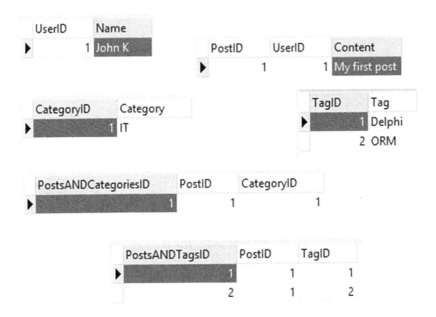

Figure 1-2. *Simplified database design and content for a blog site*

This situation looks very different for a code developer who follows OOP principles. The problem of keeping track of the users and their posts becomes a problem of defining objects and the tags and categories of the posts becomes a problem of choosing the right data structure of the programming language that can hold this information and link it back to the posts. In Delphi, and in most of the developed languages, Users and Posts would be pure objects (TUser and TPost, respectively), whereas Tags and Categories can be a list of strings represented by properties in the TPost object. The following code demonstrates this approach:

```
type
  TUser = class
  private
    fName: string;
  public
    property Name: string read fName write fName;
  end;
```

```
TPost = class
private
  FCategories: TList<string>;
  FContent: string;
  FTags: TList<string>;
  FUser: TUser;
public
  property Categories: TList<string> read fCategories write
  fCategories;
  property Content: string read fContent write fContent;
  property Tags: TList<string> read fTags write fTags;
  property User: TUser read fUser write fUser;
end;
```

This snippet suggests that if a developer wants to store data in a database and, consequently, retrieve it, they must figure out how a TList<string> or a TUser data type in TPost translates efficiently and reliably to database tables. Moreover, the situation can increase in complexity if one considers that the tags and categories can be objects themselves (TTag and TCategory), which makes the TList<string> a TObjectList<TTag> and TObjectList<TCategory>, respectively.

The preceding challenge of making two incompatible systems to seamlessly communicate is amplified when one realizes the wide range of database solutions that exist in the market both in the proprietary and open source domains. The vast majority of RDBMS databases today use SQL as the standard language to manipulate data. A closer look indicates that although SQL is a standardized language, different database vendors introduce their own SQL variations, constraints, and extensions apart from the basic set of commands. This, in turn, means that the developer who wants to manage TPost(s) in a database needs to be aware of the underlying database engine and perhaps make adjustments when the database is replaced by a different one.

Manipulating objects at database level introduces two more problems that need to be resolved if OOP and databases are expected to work reliably and correctly. One of the fundamental features of databases is their ability to facilitate the access of data by multiple users and at the same time (concurrency). For the OOP developer, the access of data by multiple users poses the need of synchronizing the changes being made at database level with any instances of the objects at programming level and vice versa. In the preceding example, an instance of TPost will have a set of tags in the Tags property. If a user adds a new tag and assigns it to the specific TPost instance, the communication between the OOP version of the model and the database should update the instance of TPost and perhaps the Tags property. Similarly, if the code that uses the TPost instance allows the user to add a new tag and assign it to the property Tags of this particular instance, the database tables should be updated accordingly.

Concurrency, on the other hand, opens the possibility of corrupted or partially saved data to the database. What may happen, especially in environments where multiple people access the same database assets at the same time, is that the users may edit the same piece of information for the same record at the same time. This situation, in conjunction with the previous one, can lead to challenges for the OOP developer.

ORM Frameworks

The previous discussion makes clear the fact that working out the mentioned issues requires a substantial effort at the coding side. People very often take the task of writing their own libraries to manage this situation but soon realize that the task is not a trivial one as the details can be quite complex and time-consuming. The solution to this problem is to use dedicated libraries known as object relational mapping (ORM) frameworks.

ORM frameworks provide a middle layer between object-oriented code and database operations (Hibernate, n.d.). They take the task of adapting typical objects to forms that can be understood by database engines, and they perform operations at both sides of the equation. These tools create a set of virtual object database that map classic database structures, can be understood by developers, and behave as expected in an OOP environment. They also expose a form of API that allows typical operations in a database to be performed at coding level and, in terms of database connectivity, they do a great job to abstract the underlying database engine.

In a typical three-tier application where there is a separation between the presentation, the business, and the data layers, ORM frameworks lie inside the data layer (Figure 1-3) and, contrary to the common presentation in books and articles, ORM frameworks can handle multiple database sources.

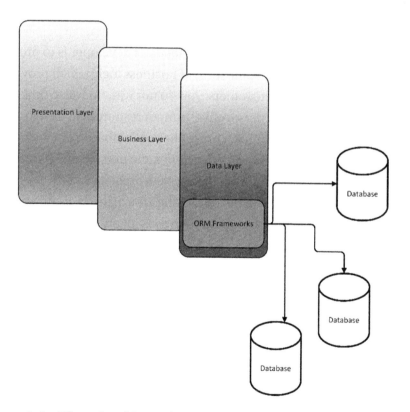

Figure 1-3. *The role of ORM frameworks in three-tier applications*

The obvious advantage of ORM frameworks is to make the life of the developers easier as they now can focus on implementing the business logic their applications dictate rather than spending time on the technical side of the storage mechanism.

ORM approaches are not without criticism. Although they are valuable solutions, they have attracted negative comments by developers on the basis of the complexity ORM introduces in its own right and the fact that once an ORM framework is used, the code is tightly coupled with it and carries all the trade-offs a specific ORM solution brings. I encourage you to do your own investigation as there are many good posts on the merits and drawbacks of ORM (Atwood, 2006; Fowler, 2012). The more you know about the tools you use, the better you position yourself to take advantage of those tools; and this is a general advice that goes beyond the scope of ORM libraries.

The reality of the matter is that if your focus as developer is to produce applications that implement some form of business logic which provides value to your business and customers, you do not want to waste time, effort, and, from company's perspective, human resources to develop your own solution that deals with the technicalities of databases. On the other hand, if you are an ORM framework developer, the perspective is totally different. ORM provides solutions to nearly 80% of the tasks you need to accomplish at database level. If the remaining 20% of the tasks make a significant difference to your business, then most likely you are part of a team that develops frameworks.

ORM Terminology

In the field of ORM, there are a number of terms that we come across repeatedly. Many terms originate from the ORM designers, and others are borrowed from the world of databases. This section provides a summary of the most commonly used terms in ORM solutions.

Entity

An *entity* is the complete set of data held by an application object as defined by the developer in order to serve the needs of a specific application. This data set replicates the data found in the underlying database. A customer, an employee, or the blog posts from the previous example are typical representatives of an entity. In the code, the objects may hold more data and exhibit additional functionality than what is required at database level, but the idea is that when you look at an entity in the code, you have at the very minimum access to all the data in the database that this entity is associated to. For the database administrator, entities usually match to tables in the database, and an instance of the object (entity) in the code corresponds to a row (record) in that table.

Additionally, entities in code are used for other purposes than just to simply represent records in a table in the database. In databases, very often designers encapsulate a logical perspective of data that requires the combination of data found within different tables using keys and other database elements. Quite often, this logic also dictates the need for a range of calculations. In databases, this representation is implemented by *views,* and at code level entities are used for this purpose as well.

Properties

Entity's data is stored in *properties* in the same way that classic objects use properties to hold data. As mentioned earlier, entities match database tables and table records; therefore, those instances should be uniquely identifiable by the ORM framework at the entity level. This is resolved by assigning a property to act as unique identifier. This concept is basically the same as the idea of primary keys in databases. One difference between properties in entities and the underlying data in databases is that the first ones can hold simple or complex data types.

Associations

Entities, like tables in databases, are generated in order to support a model that derives from a business problem. Entities make sense in a model when they form relationships that represent logical and conceptual notions. These relationships are called *associations* in ORM frameworks, and they are formed between one or more properties.

These properties in the ORM space are known as association endpoints, and depending on the data types they can define the different types of associations (cardinality) as represented by the common one-to-one, one-to-many, and many-to-many relationships. Although one-to-one and many-to-many relationships can be described in theoretical terms and implemented at database level, they hardly make business sense. Therefore, in most of the entity frameworks, all associations represent one-to-many (and vice versa) relationships, and if other relationship cardinalities (one-to-one) are required, it is left to the developer to enforce and filter them out.

Associations are always bidirectional so entities have full access to each other. In many ways, at database level, endpoint properties work in the same way as foreign keys do, and they behave in a way similar to joined table operations.

Criteria

When developers want to fetch data from databases, they create query statements using the relevant (SQL) language. The statements may or may not filter the results of the query. At ORM level, queries are built based on conditions that are passed to the underlying database engine. These conditions, which can be generic or specific, are formed by attaching *criteria* together. Most ORM frameworks provide a fluent interface (Ramsay, 2008) to manage criteria (meaning that the building of the query statement appears as a natural language to the user), and you can typically expect to have criteria for all the useful relational comparisons (e.g., greater than, equal, logical and, logical or, etc.) and sorting functions for properties.

Projections

Although you can retrieve all the properties (columns) of a table data from a database using ORM criteria, common programming practice indicates that you should only fetch the properties that are required in each situation. This type of queries is managed differently by ORM packages than the typical criteria-based queries, and they are called *projections*. Projections also allow programmers to drill down complicated data structures and even perform some (basic) mathematical calculations (e.g., average, summation, etc.).

Container

ORM frameworks create a buffer between the code and the database. When the user passes an operation to the ORM, the framework needs to have access to the status of all of the data in the database. The framework loads the relevant data in the memory in the form of entities or other relevant data structures, performs the instructed operations, and then, many times, pushes back the changes to the database. This snapshot of the data is managed by an *entity container*. Before the developer can interact with an entity, ORM libraries load any required data into a container. The containers are usually short-lived as their purpose is to serve a specific set of operations and lightweight as they need to be created and destroyed several times in the life of an application. In many aspects, a container is somewhat analogous to a database transaction.

The typical course of action in an ORM is as follows:

- The developer creates an instance of the container. The container is also known as *entity manager,* and the instance of the manager is sometimes referred to as the *context.*

- The developer uses the container to perform operations to entities. The operations may require interaction with the database as in the case of updating an entity or may only retrieve results like in the case of a query.

- Once the operations are completed, the entity container (manager) is destroyed.

Putting It All Together

Figure 1-4 shows the several elements discussed earlier and their connection to the database structure based on the blog site example.

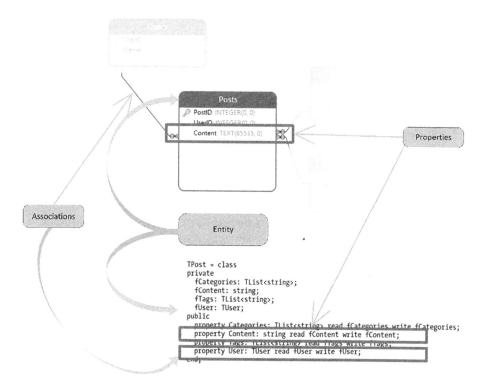

Figure 1-4. *Various elements of ORM frameworks and their relationship to database structure*

Figure 1-5 pictures the ideas of criteria, projection, and entity container providing sample code.

Figure 1-5. *Sample code to demonstrate the concepts of criteria, projection, and entity container in ORM frameworks*

Workflows

Depending on the available resources and information, several workflows can be devised that lead to a specific goal. In the area of ORM frameworks, there are three main workflow patterns[1]:

- Code-first

- Model-first

- Database-first

Each of the preceding workflows becomes productive under specific conditions and meets specific needs. In general, these workflows attempt to make the work of the developer more structured and allow them to focus on how to build an application which adds business value rather than lock the developer in deep technical mazes indirectly linked to the goal of the application.

Code-First Workflow

This approach is relevant when you have an existing application and a point comes in the development life where persistence becomes a requirement. You typically follow OOP approaches and your application uses classes extensively. In the initial stages, the code does not consider any ORM framework requirements, conventions, or techniques. The database is created based on the class design, and the developer has full control on the way the ORM will generate the database structure. It offers flexibility but it requires more work to set the classes up correctly.

Code-first approach may be effective in small teams of developers or in the case of a sole developer, but it does not work well with large developer

---

[1]These workflows were introduced and promoted by Microsoft's Entity Framework at different stages and releases (Microsoft, 2016).

teams because it opens the possibilities for inconsistencies in class design. For this reason, it requires central management of the fundamental classes of the application. Additionally, code-first workflow can be used in applications that have a database already, but an additional step is required where the developer must reverse engineer the database and produce the appropriate classes.

As an example, the code snippet in the blog case represents the code-first approach. The developer defines the classes first and the ORM generates the database.

In this book, we are going to start with the code-first approach because it allows the exploration of different approaches and it encourages more in-depth understanding of the framework.

Model-First Workflow

The model-first approach assumes that the application requires a persistent medium and database support from the outset. When developers design the model first, they abstract the storage mechanism by focusing on the design of the database. Typically, a graphical environment is used as a tool to generate the underlying classes. Figure 1-1 represents the model of the blog application.

This approach is useful when someone works in a new application or in an application that does not have any databases yet. Additionally, the use of graphical elements creates a prototype of the database, and this proves to be a useful tool when it comes to sharing ideas and approaches between members of teams or between development groups.

As mentioned, code-first is the approach we are going to focus on in this book when we build our ORM entities. In Chapter 8 we are going to explore a separate tool called Data Modeler, which allows us to follow the model-first approach.

Database-First Workflow

This approach is based on existing databases. The framework can generate classes that match the database entities and relationships and, then, developers interact with these classes. This is appropriate when a new application needs to be developed based on existing data. This situation is common in software development and leads to the model-first approach.

Database-first development does not put any constraints in terms of the number of databases the framework uses. Although the workflow comes with the assumption of one database in use, the approach can be used with multiple databases. ORM frameworks are capable of managing more than one databases.

The biggest advantage of this approach is the consistency in the generation of the classes in the ORM framework (Smartbear, 2013). This makes the approach suitable to large teams where different groups may design and work in different parts of a database. This approach will generate a very consistent class tree that can be shared among the team members. On the other hand, it offers limited flexibility as the developers do not have the opportunity to alter the class design because the next update to the database and, consequently, to the classes will overwrite any changes.

As with the case of the model-first design, we are going to look at this approach with Data Modeler in Chapter 8.

Choosing Workflows

The available workflows are useful in many different circumstances, but they generally describe a dedicated approach to achieving a goal. This means that, in theory, one would choose a workflow and stick with it. However, real-life work environments are hardly pure (Microsoft, 2016), and it is typical to mix and match workflows. For example, you may start a new application with the code-first approach and as the complexity increases you may find it more productive to move to a model-first workflow.

Summary

This chapter provides an introduction to object relational mapping frameworks. A discussion of the fundamental ideas and concepts puts light to the way these frameworks are designed, and different workflows associated with ORM libraries are discussed. This chapter offers the basic knowledge that allows us to, firstly, explore TMS Aurelius ORM in Delphi and, secondly, to work in developing an example application.

References

Atwood, J., 2006. *Object-Relational Mapping is the Vietnam of Computer Science.* [Online] Available at: `https://blog.codinghorror.com/object-relational-mapping-is-the-vietnam-of-computer-science/` [Accessed 28 02 2019].

Fowler, M., 2012. *Martin Fowler on ORM Hate.* [Online] Available at: `https://dzone.com/articles/martin-fowler-orm-hate` [Accessed 28 02 2019].

Hibernate, n.d.. *What is Object/Relational Mapping.* [Online] Available at: `http://hibernate.org/orm/what-is-an-orm/` [Accessed 28 02 2019].

Microsoft, 2016. *Get started with Entity Framework 6.* [Online] Available at: `https://docs.microsoft.com/en-us/ef/ef6/get-started` [Accessed 28 02 2019].

Mueller, J. P., 2013. *Microsoft ADO.NET Entity Framework.* California: O'Reilly Media, Inc..

Ramsay, C., 2008. *NHibernate: Optimising Queries with Projections*. [Online] Available at: http://colinramsay.co.uk/nhibernate/2008/01/15/nhibernate-optimising-queries-with-projections.html [Accessed 28 02 2019].

Smartbear, 2013. *Choosing the Right Entity Framework Workflow*. [Online] Available at: https://smartbear.com/blog/develop/choosing-the-right-entity-framework-workflow/ [Accessed 29 02 2019].

CHAPTER 2

TMS Aurelius

TMS Aurelius is an ORM framework for Delphi developers. The framework is written in Delphi, and it is a proprietary product developed by TMS Software. Aurelius has been available in the market for a number of years, and it enjoys a good customer base. The framework plays its part in a wide range of applications with different scope and different requirements. Aurelius is not limited to Windows platforms, and it can work efficiently on macOS, iOS, Android, and Linux, and it supports all Delphi versions from XE2 to the latest.

In this chapter, we start clean and install Aurelius from scratch. Then, the chapter explores some fundamental concepts (database connectivity, SQL dialects, etc.) that allow us to use Aurelius, and we look at our first code snippets that put Aurelius to work for us.

Installation

Aurelius comes in two versions: a trial version and a licensed one. The difference is that with the trial version you only get the DCU files; it is intended for noncommercial use and it expires at some point. There is a free version as well which does not expire and you can use it for commercial applications, but there are some limitations. For more information about the free version, contact TMS Software directly. The next steps guide you how to install the trial and the licensed versions.

© John Kouraklis 2019

J. Kouraklis, *Introducing Delphi ORM*, https://doi.org/10.1007/978-1-4842-5013-6_2

Trial Version

In you want to install the trial version, follow the next steps:

1. Go to the product's web page on TMS Software site at this address `https://tmssoftware.com/site/aurelius.asp` or visit `https://tmssoftware.com` and select "Business Tools" from the tiles with their products. This will load a page with several interesting pieces of information. At the bottom of the page, you can find the link to access the Aurelius web page.

2. In Aurelius page, scroll at the bottom of the page. You will be able to see a grayed area with download links for different Delphi versions (Figure 2-1). Select the link for the Delphi version you use and download the file in your computer.

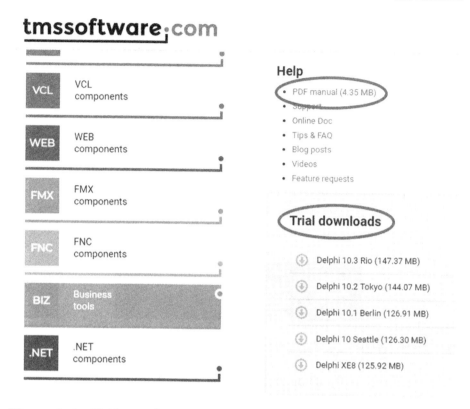

Figure 2-1. *TMS Aurelius trial download links*

Note   In the same page you can also find the technical manual, as shown in Figure 2-1. This is also copied by the installer, but if you wish to have the manual without installing the package, download it from the link.

3.   The downloaded file is a compressed zip file that contains all the products in the TMS Business Tools package. Extract the files and execute the installer.

4.   Let the installer complete the installation of all packages.

5. If you haven't changed the default location, Aurelius is now installed in `Documents\tmssoftware\ businessrio\Aurelius`.

    Note: The `businessrio` part in the preceding path indicates the Delphi version you install the package for. In my case, I installed Aurelius for Delphi 10.3 Rio.

6. Now, you can launch Delphi and check that the package has been installed correctly. In the splash screen, you should be able to see the BIZ logo and a reference to the package similar to Figure 2-2.

Figure 2-2. *Splash screen item for Aurelius trial version (Delphi 10.3 Rio)*

7. Additionally, if you look at the `Options` ➤ `Library` paths for different platforms, you should be able to see the paths to the compiled packages (Figure 2-3).

8. Now, you are ready to use Aurelius in your Delphi programs.

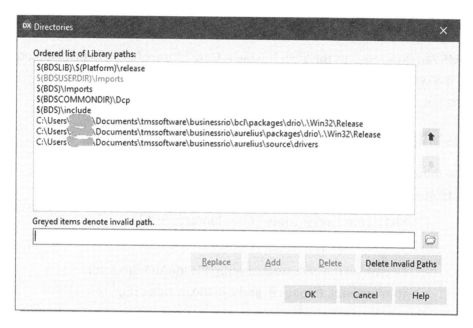

Figure 2-3. *Library paths for Aurelius trial version (Win32)*

Note   The trial version of the package installs compiled `.dcu` units for all the available platforms and for the `Release` configuration. Source files for several database drivers have also been installed. Additionally, you can find `Demos` and `Documentation` in their respective folders.

Licensed Version

If you are a registered user with TMS Software, you can log in to your account in their web site. In your account, you are able to download all the products you have purchased license for. Note that licensed installers build packages for all the installed Delphi version in your system, eliminating the need to run separate installation for each Delphi IDE.

Prerequisite Packages

TMS Aurelius requires the TMS Business Core Library (BCL) to be installed in the system. Download the compressed setup file from your account, unzip it, and install the package.

Installation

The following steps describe how you can install the registered version of TMS Aurelius:

1. Make sure TMS Business Core Library (BCL) is installed (see previous section).

2. Download the compressed setup file for Aurelius from your account, unpack it, and run the installer (Figure 2-4).

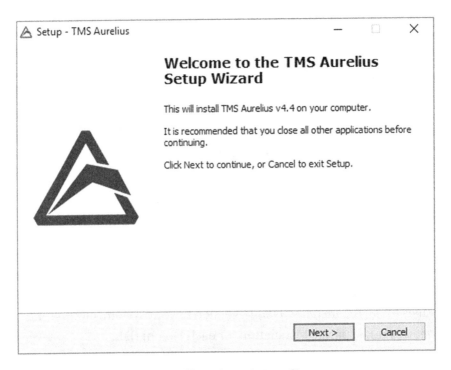

Figure 2-4. *Registered installer of TMS Aurelius*

3. The next page in the installer invites you to accept the license, and then you have to enter your registration email and code (supplied by TMS). This step requires your system to be able to access the Internet as the installer validates your license online.

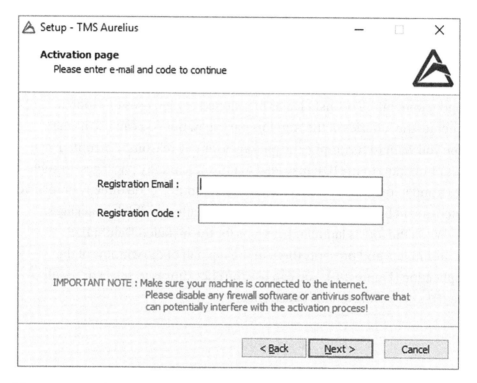

Figure 2-5. *License page in TMS Aurelius installer*

4. Verify the settings that are presented in the following pages of the installer and allow it to copy all the necessary files to your system.

5. When all files are copied, the installer will launch the Package Rebuild Tool to build the packages for all the installed Delphi versions and all available releases. For more details, see the next section.

6. When the building of the package finishes, Aurelius is installed and it is ready to use. You should be able to see the TMS Business product line logo in the Delphi splash screen as in Figure 2-2 and also inspect the relevant library paths.

Package Rebuild Tool

The Package Rebuild Tool is a stand-alone application that is installed with TMS Aurelius. You can find it in the Start Menu group and launch it independently. The installer, as mentioned earlier, uses this tool to generate the binaries of the Aurelius packages, but you can use it every time you want to recompile the packages for any reasons. Corrupted .dcu files or updates to the IDE may lead to unusable binary packages. In such cases and in the cases where you modify the source code directly or receive patches sent by TMS Software, you can manually rebuild the packages.

When the tool is launched, it scans for the installed Delphi IDE environments and presents them in the top half of the window of the application (Figure 2-6). You can use the checkboxes to select or deselect the IDEs according to your preference.

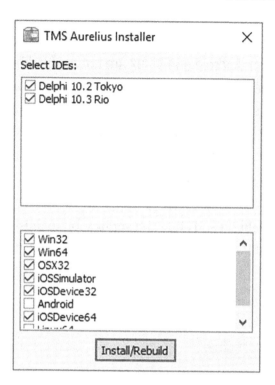

Figure 2-6. *The Package Rebuild Tool*

At the bottom half of the window, the available platforms are shown, and you can select which ones you would like to install or rebuild the packages for. This part of the user interface can be confusing as the design indicates that the platform selection is independent to the Delphi version. For example, if I want to build the packages for OSX32 for Delphi 10.2 but not for Delphi 10.3, I need to rebuild the packages twice; one for 10.2 with OSX32 selected and one for 10.3 with OSX32 deselected.

Note   Figure 2-6 demonstrates a very common situation with the available platform. Android and Linux are not enabled because the tool identifies these platforms either as wrongly configured or not available. In my system, Linux is not available as built platform and Android is not properly configured. If you have the same situation, check the SDK Manager in Delphi, correct any errors that appear, and rerun the Package Rebuild Tool.

Click Install/Rebuild and allow the application to finish the building of the packages (Figure 2-7). This step may take considerable amount of time to complete.

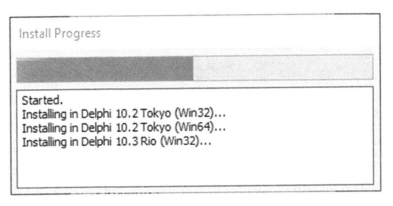

Figure 2-7. *The Package Rebuild Tools compiling for several Delphi versions and platforms*

TMS Subscription Manager

TMS Software offers a simpler and more automated way to manage any packages you have purchased. As a registered user, you have access to a tool called TMS Subscription Manager. This tool allows you to keep track of the installed packages and see new versions, and it facilitates the installation (and uninstallation) of the packages.

In the case of Aurelius and Business Core Library, the Subscription Manager would look like in Figure 2-8. The Manager shows that there are new versions available and they can be, automatically, downloaded and installed.

Figure 2-8. *TMS Subscription Manager*

Database Connectivity

Aurelius can connect to a number of database engines. The framework requires the following elements in order to manage an underlying database:

- A component that actually allows Aurelius to access the database. There are two ways for this to be defined:

  - **Using an *adapter* (Adapter Mode)**: The adapter works as a proxy between Aurelius and a database, and it requires components by the providers of the adapter to be installed and configured properly. This option provides high flexibility and great degree of customization of the connection. FireDAC component belongs in this group.

  - **Using a *native driver* (Driver Mode)**: This mode provides a convenient way to use a database in Aurelius without the need to install or employ any third-party software as in the *adapter* mode. Although the flexibility in customization is not as high as in adapter mode, this mode is a very convenient and quick way to set up the database connectivity of the framework. In the version of Aurelius at the time of writing, this mode allows native connectivity to SQLite databases and databases hosted by Microsoft SQL Server.

- **An SQL Dialect**: When Aurelius gets the connection, it needs to know which variation of the SQL language should be used to communicate with the database. This information is passed by supplying an SQL dialect during the database connectivity setup stage. The ability to define the dialect is exposed to the developers

only in the case of the adapter mode. In the native
driver mode, Aurelius can work out the required dialect
by looking at the selected native driver.

Table 2-1 shows which components can be used to connect to specific
databases. According to Aurelius manual, these are the combinations
that TMS has tested and officially supports. As the table indicates, there
are components that can be used to provide access to multiple databases.
This can be very beneficiary and convenient in cases where there is a
database change as a matter of infrastructure or your application requires
to connect to different databases. You can save writing lots of lines of
code and time if you know that a specific adapter works with different
databases. Aurelius technical manual provides a full list of the available
adapters, SQL dialects, native drivers, and which component and
database versions are supported.

IDBConnection

In terms of coding, *a connection to a database* in Aurelius is represented
by the IDBConnection interface. This interface is perhaps one of the
most fundamental data structures in Aurelius as it makes the database
operations happen. The adapters or the drivers discussed in the previous
section are used to create a valid IDBConnection interface. In turn, this
means that an IDBConnection is tied to an adapter or a driver and not to a
database engine (although when you use an adapter that can access only
one database, then the IDBConnection is ultimately tied to one database as
well), and this is

Table 2-1. *Databases and Connection Adapter Compatibility (Homologation) in TMS Aurelius*

Database \ Adapter	Native	Absolute	AnyDAC	dbExpres	dbGo	DOA	ElevateDB	FireDAC	FIBPlus	IBO	IBX	NativeDB	NexusDB	SQLDirect	UniDAC	UIB	ZeosDB
AbsoluteDB		●															
IBM DB2			●		●			●						●	●		
ElevateDB							●										
FireBird (including FireBird 3)			●	●				●	●	●					●	●	●
Interbase			●	●				●		●	●				●	●	
MS SQL Server	●		●	●	●			●						●	●		●
MySQL			●	●				●						●	●		●
NexusDB													●				
Oracle			●	●		●		●						●	●		●
PostgreSQL			●					●							●		
SQLAnywhere								●				●					
SQLite	●		●					●							●		

where the value of having adapter that are able to access multiple databases appears. There are three ways to instantiate an `IDBConnection` interface:

1. Using pure code

2. Using the `TAureliusConnection` component

3. Using the TMS Aurelius DBConnection wizard in RAD IDE

Using Code

To demonstrate how we can get an `IDBConnection` programmatically, we'll create a connection to an SQLite database. Table 2-1 indicates that this can be achieved in Aurelius by either using a database adapter or natively. For this example, we are going to create an in-memory SQLite database.

Using an Adapter

Let's start with an adapter:

1. Create a new project in Delphi. It can be a VCL, FMX, or console application, but it is much easier if you choose a VCL or FMX project.

2. Drop a FireDAC connection (`TFDConnection`) in the form (`FDConnection1`).

3. Select the connection component, right-click, and launch the connection editor (Figure 2-9). Select *SQLite* in *Driver ID* field and enter "*:memory:*" in the *Database* field as in the figure and choose OK.

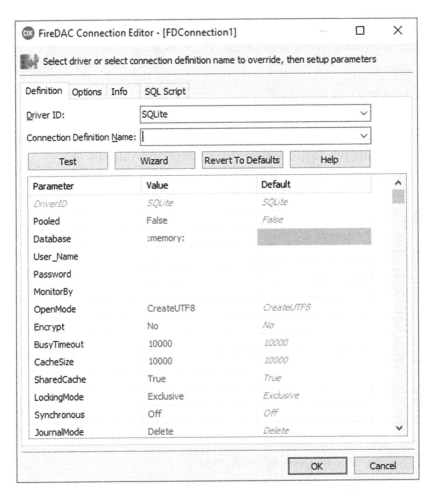

Figure 2-9. *FireDAC Connection Editor for in-memory SQLite database*

4. Click the OnCreate event of the form and write the
   following code:

```
uses
  ...,
  Aurelius.Drivers.Interfaces;

type
  TForm1 = class(TForm)
    FDConnection1: TFDConnection;
    procedure FormCreate(Sender: TObject);
  private
    fConnection: IDBConnection;
  public
    { Public declarations }
  end;

var
  Form1: TForm1;

implementation

uses
  Aurelius.Drivers.FireDac;

{$R *.fmx}

procedure TForm1.FormCreate(Sender: TObject);
begin
  fConnection:=TFireDacConnectionAdapter.Create(FDConnection1,
  false);
end;
```

This will create an
IDBConnection based on
the FireDAC component

After the call to the TFireDacConnectionAdapter constructor, the
fConnection property holds a reference to the database and can be used to
perform operations.

Using Native Drivers

As mentioned earlier, Aurelius can provide native support to SQLite databases. This means that there is no need to create a FireDAC connection. Aurelius can access directly the SQLite database as shown in the code that follows:

```
...

implementation

uses
  Aurelius.Drivers.SQLite;

...

procedure TForm1.FormCreate(Sender: TObject);
begin
  fConnection:=TSQLiteNativeConnectionAdapter.Create(':memory:');
end;
```

Note   The native component is very useful as it requires the minimal possible code to generate a database connection and does not require any third-party components. However, it does not provide a way to access encrypted SQLite databases. If you want to achieve this, you need to use a FireDAC component.

Using the `TAureliusConnection` Component

Aurelius provides a design-time component that can be used with a FireDAC connection.

1.   Create a new project in Delphi.

2. Drop a FireDAC connection (TFDConnection) in the
    form (FDConnection1) as before.

3. Drop a TAureliusConnection component in the
    form (AureliusConnection1). You should be able to
    see two components as in Figure 2-10.

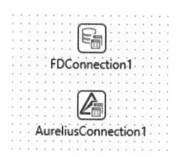

Figure 2-10. *FireDAC and Aurelius connections in a form*

4. Select the Aurelius connection component, right-
    click, and select *"Connection Settings..."*. In the
    editor make the necessary options to connect to
    the FireDAC component (Figure 2-11) and select
    OK. You can also test the connection using the
    button at the bottom of the form.

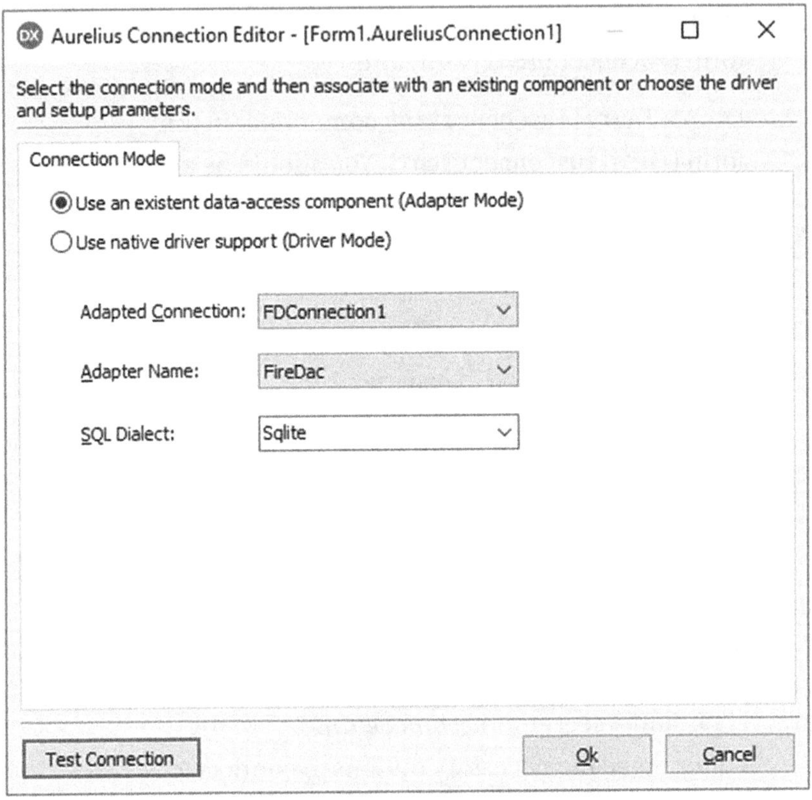

Figure 2-11. *TAureliusConnection Connection Editor*

5. Retrieve the IDBConnection using the following code:

```
procedure TForm1.FormCreate(Sender: TObject);
begin
  fConnection:=AureliusConnection1.CreateConnection;
end;
```

Using the TMS Aurelius DBConnection Wizard

TMS provides an even easier way to generate a database connection. Aurelius installer adds a DBConnection wizard in the *File➤New➤Other➤TMS Business* menu in the RAD Studio.

1. Go to *File* ➤ *New* ➤ *Other* ➤ *TMS Business* in Delphi and select the TMS Aurelius DBConnection wizard as in Figure 2-12.

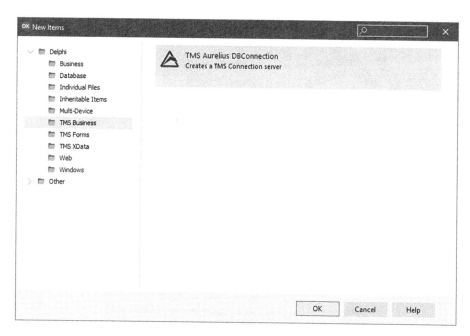

Figure 2-12. *TMS Aurelius DBConnection option in Delphi*

2. In the next step (Figure 2-13), choose whether you want to connect to the database using an adapter or a native driver. For this example, I opted for the native driver to generate an SQLite database.

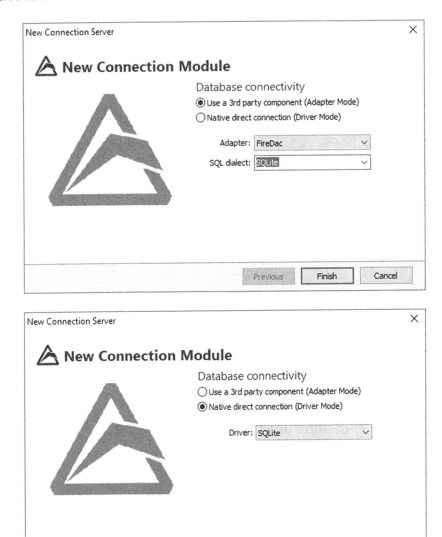

Figure 2-13. *The options in DBConnection wizard for the adapter and the driver modes*

3. The wizard creates a unit (ConnectionModule.pas) with a data module and a TAureliusConnection attached to it. The name of the module is after the connection. In my case, it is called TSQLiteSQLiteConnection and the associated variable is SQLiteSQLiteConnection. This naming convention may appear confusing to the Delphi developer as the name implies that the underlying object is a connection when it is, actually, a data module. This may not be a big problem because the only real need for this module is to generate an IDBConnection instance once. In a typical application, this will most likely be done at the beginning of the application, and the interface will be injected as needed.

4. Once the data module is created and the Aurelius connection has been configured, the connection interface can be retrieved as in the following code. Note that the wizard assigns a variable to the data module, but it is not instantiated. This needs to be done manually.

...

```
implementation

uses
  ...,
  ConnectionModule;
```

Instantiate the data module

```
...

procedure TForm1.FormCreate(Sender: TObject);
begin

SQLiteSQLiteConnection:=TSQLiteSQLiteConnection.Create(self);
  fConnection:=SQLiteSQLiteConnection.CreateConnection;
end;
```

Retrieve the IDBConnection

ORM Paradigm in Aurelius

In the previous chapter, the ORM building elements were discussed (entity, properties, associations, criteria, projections, container). In order for Aurelius to implement these elements, the framework defines a number of attributes that can be used.

The attributes determine how the virtual object database in Aurelius is defined and managed and how the operations at the database level are performed. They also work as indicators in the code. If you browse through the code, you can understand the ORM structure by observing the attributes. To demonstrate the use of attributes in Aurelius, we will continue with the blog example from the first chapter.

Note   If you are not familiar with attributes in Delphi or you would like a refresher, visit the official Delphi documentation (Embarcadero, n.d.). For a more detailed treatment of attributes, you may find useful to check Nick Hodges' book (Hodges, 2014).

Entity

Entities in ORM frameworks are represented by classes and their instances. In Aurelius, you declare a class to be an entity for the framework and, therefore, persistent in the database, by using the attribute [Entity]. In this case, the TPost class is declared to be an entity by, simply, writing the following code:

```
[Entity]
TPost = class
private
  FCategories: TList<string>;
  FContent: string;
```

```
  FTags: TList<string>;
  FUser: TUser;
public
  property Categories: TList<string> read FCategories write
  FCategories;
  property Content: string read FContent write FContent;
  property Tags: TList<string> read FTags write FTags;
  property User: TUser read FUser write FUser;
end;
```

This attribute tells Aurelius that TPost class exists in the underlying database. The next step is to decorate the class with the [Table] attribute and the desired name of the table.

```
[Entity]
[Table('Posts')]
TPost = class
  ...
end;
```

Aurelius knows that it has to include in the virtual object database any class with the [Entity] attribute. However, at the initial stages of your code and if you follow the model-first or code-first workflow, you may declare classes that are not used anywhere in the code yet. This results in the classes being removed during the compilation and linking phase in Delphi.

As a result, those classes will not appear as tables in the underlying databases as Aurelius will not know that those classes exist. Initially, this may not pose a real concern because the next time you use the class, the linker will include it to the executable and Aurelius will update the database schema accordingly. Problems may arise when associations exist between classes that represent association endpoints where one endpoint is used in the application and another one is not yet. This will make the final executable to link only the classes from the endpoints that are used, leaving the associations at Aurelius level in nonfunctional state.

In order to avoid this situation, which, admittedly, may be a headache to debug, best practice indicates that you register the classes right at the beginning of the application. This is typically done by using the RegisterEntity procedure in the initialization section of a unit or as the very first line an application executes. For the TPost entity, this would look like the following code:

```
uses
  ...,
  Aurelius.Mapping.Attributes;

type
  [Entity]
  [Table('Posts')]
  TPost = class
    ...
  end;

...

initialization
...
  RegisterEntity(TPost) ;
...
end.
```

Properties

Properties in ORM represent columns in database tables and are mapped in typical class properties in Delphi implemented by either a (usually private) field or a field and a getter and setter method. From Aurelius' point of view, properties (with the exception of associations) can be of four types:

1. Identifier

2. Column

3. Column (NULL)

4. Blob

Identifier

Each entity in Aurelius should be, uniquely, identified in the framework as a record is, uniquely, identified in a table by a primary key. This is done by declaring a property of the class to use the [Id] attribute. The most common approach here is to allow the database to manage the generation of the identifier value as in the case of a primary key. This is not restrictive as you can take control of the values of the identifier and manage it in your code. Typical values include sequential numbers, but for our TPost I will use a GUID as identifier as this approach is gradually becoming more common among database engineers.

```
[Entity]
[Table('Post')]
[Id('FID', TIdGenerator.SmartGuid)]          fID reference to
TPost = class                                allow Aurelius to
private                                       declare an
  [Column('ID', [TColumnProp.Required])]     identifier
  FID: TGuid;
  ...
public
  property ID: TGuid read FID write FID;
  ...
end;
```

The code defines a new property ID of TGUID type and the corresponding private variable (fID). The [Id] attribute is used to declare to Aurelius that fID is the variable to be used as the identifier of the class and that Aurelius will need to generate GUID identifiers. There are more identifier engines available, and they are discussed in the manual.

If you need to declare composite identifiers in your database, just add as many [Id] properties as required. In that case, Aurelius will completely manage the generation of the identifier so the engine in the attribute should be TIdGenerator.None. However, broadly speaking, the official manual suggests that composite identifiers should be avoided.

Column

Each property in a class that needs to be persistent in the database corresponds to a column in the equivalent table. In Aurelius, the [Column] attribute is used to declare a column. When an identifier is declared, the column in the table should never be empty (null). This is passed to Aurelius by using the TColumnProp.Required in the declaration of the [Column] property and can be seen in the preceding code snippet. As an example, we are going to add a property DateTime in TPost of TDateTime.

```
[Entity]
[Table('Post')]
[Id('FID', TIdGenerator.SmartGuid)]
TPost = class
private
  ...
  [Column('DateTime', [TColumnProp.Required])]
  fDateTime: TDateTime;
  ...
public
  ...
  property DateTime: TDateTime read FDateTime write FDateTime;
  ...
end;
```

Note that the DateTime field has been declared as *NOT NULL* (*required*) in the database. If you want to declare the length of a field or its precision for numeric fields (columns), the [Column] attribute receives parameters that can accommodate these requirements. The manual provides more details on this.

Column (NULL)

In databases, columns can be empty *(NULL)*, a concept that is different from empty fields in classes. For example, in TPost, the Content field is a string. An empty string field in the class yields length of 0; however, a null column in the database table does not as it does not have any content. This situation is managed by Aurelius with the introduction of the generic record Nullable<T> and it is used as in the following code. Note that I have declared the length of the column to 65535 which is the maximum value for VarChar in SQLite, but this seems a poor choice for full-scale production database.

```
uses
  ...,
  Aurelius.Types.Nullable;

...

[Entity]
[Table('Post')]
[Id('FID', TIdGenerator.SmartGuid)]
TPost = class
private
  ...
  [Column('Content', [], 65535)]
  FContent: Nullable<string>;
  ...
public
  ...
    property Content: Nullable<string> read FContent write
FContent;
  ...
end;
```

Property Content converted to Nullable<string>

Blob

Databases are capable of storing binary large objects (blobs) , and Aurelius naturally provides support to such data types by introducing the TBlob record. This is pretty straightforward to use in an entity. As an example, we introduce an Image property in TPost to hold a picture related to the post.

```
uses
  ...,
  Aurelius.Types.Blob;

...

[Entity]
[Table('Post')]
[Id('FID', TIdGenerator.SmartGuid)]
TPost = class
private
  ...
  [Column('Image', [TColumnProp.Lazy])]
  FImage: TBlob;
public
  ...
  property Image: TBlob read FImage write FImage;
end;
```

The [Column] attribute provides a way to affect the behavior of TBlob. In the example code, the FImage field will not be loaded immediately when a Post instance (record) is retrieved in the code (lazy loading); instead the content will become available the very first moment the Image property is accessed. This is common behavior with blobs. We will also see this behavior again when we deal with associations.

Associations

As discussed in the previous chapter, associations are formed between endpoints (properties in entities). Aurelius implements two types of associations: one-to-many and many-to-one. If you need to implement one-to-one associations, you need to handle this by code.

According to our design, a user in our blog case owns several posts. From the user's point of view, this is a one-to-many association. On the other hand, looking at the situation from a post and considering the previous association, the relationship between a post and a user is many-to-one (Figure 2-14).

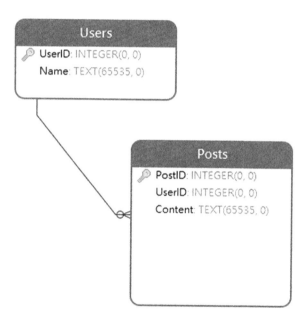

Figure 2-14. *Users and posts associations*

Many-to-One Association

A TUser is the owner of a specific post; therefore, this entity deserves a property in TPost. Typically, in an OOP fashion, we would call this property User. Then, we need to tell Aurelius that this property relates to the entity TUser. We accomplish this by decorating the corresponding field of User property with the [Association] attribute.

```
[Entity]
[Table('Post')]
[Id('FID', TIdGenerator.SmartGuid)]
TPost = class
private
  ...
  [Association([], CascadeTypeAll - [TCascadeType.Remove])]
  [JoinColumn('User', [], 'ID')]
  FUser: TUser;
public
  ...
  property User: TUser read FUser write FUser;
end;
```

The Association attribute tells Aurelius that there is a relationship between the two entities. In database theory, this refers to the concept of foreign keys. In the preceding code, I also define the behavior of the association by indicating that all changes except Remove will be cascaded by using the constant CascadeTypeAll - [TCascadeType.Remove]. Instead of this expression, I could also use the CascadeTypeAllButRemove identifier. Only with the Association attribute, Aurelius is not in the position to know which column (field) in the User table serves as the foreign key. We provide this information by using the [JoinColumn] attribute. In the preceding code, the foreign key links to the ID (primary key) column in the User table. Up to this point, we have not defined it so we add a property in TUser.

```
[Entity]
[Table('User')]
[Id('FID', TIdGenerator.SmartGuid)]
TUser = class
private
 [Column('ID', [TColumnProp.Required])]
 FID: TGuid;
 ...
public
 property ID: TGuid read FID write FID;
 ...
end;
```

It is imperative to use both these attributes together; otherwise, you will get an error. As you can see in the code, both attributes provide a way to tailor the behavior of the foreign key relationship by supplying additional parameters. The manual includes very detailed information for both attributes.

One-to-Many Association

As code-first developers, the premise that "*a user owns several posts*" is basically implemented by the use of a TList as in the following code. A new read-only property (Posts) is created to hold this list.

```
[Entity]
[Table('User')]
[Id('FID', TIdGenerator.SmartGuid)]

TUser = class
private
```

```
  ...
  FPosts: TList<TPost>;
public
  property Posts: TList<TPost> read FPosts;
end;
```

In order to create this type of association in Aurelius, we have to use the [ManyValuedAssociation] attribute. This attribute is used in two ways. If there is already an association with the other endpoint (bidirectional), you can pass the field or the property directly to the attribute as demonstrated in the following code:

```
[Entity]
[Table('User')]
[Id('FID', TIdGenerator.Guid)]
TUser = class
private
  ...
  [ManyValuedAssociation([], CascadeTypeAll], 'FUser')]
  FPosts: TList<TPost>;
public
  ...
end;
```

This tells Aurelius that the corresponding field in TPost is FUser. In other words, when Aurelius loads FPosts, it populates the list with those TPost objects that have their fUser attribute the same as the identifier FID of the current instance of TUser.

In the case where a class does not have a defined association, the same result can be achieved by supplying the [ForeignJoinColumn] attribute immediately after [ManyValuedAssociation]. More information and examples appear in the manual, but it seems that this attribute exists to cover some corner-case situations.

One-to-One Association

Aurelius does not provide a special attribute to manage one-to-one associations. This can be resolved if you see one-to-one association as one-to-many and filter the retrieval of the data to provide one and only result. To demonstrate this, let us assume that the user in our blog site can create one and only one post. The next snippet shows how we would create a one-to-one relationship:

```
[Entity]
[Table('User')]
[Id('FID', TIdGenerator.Guid)]
TUser = class
private
  ...
  [ManyValuedAssociation([], CascadeTypeAll], 'FUser')]
  fPosts: TList<TPost>;

  function getPost: TPost;
  procedure setPost (const aPost: TPost);
public
  ...
  property Post: TPost read getPost write setPost;
end;

...

function TUser.getPost: TPost;
begin
  if FPosts.Value.Count > 0 then
    result := FPosts.Value[0]
  else
    result := nil;
end;
```

```
procedure TUser.setPost (const aPost: TPost);
begin
  if FPosts.Value.Count = 0 then
    FPosts.Add(Value)
  else
    FPosts[0] := Value;
end;
```

Lazy Loading

All the previous examples are designed in such a way that when a Post is retrieved by Aurelius, the User property will get the object with the user at the same time. Similarly, when a User is loaded, the Posts property (TList) will be created and loaded with content. This is the default (eager) loading.

Although in our examples the footprint of such approach is subtle, in full-scale applications with complex databases, it will load unnecessary content stretching the available resources. The behavior of the properties can be altered to allow loading of valid content only when they are accessed (lazy loading).

Lazy loading requires a virtual proxy, a mechanism that shows the same properties as the underlying entity but controls when the loading of the actual content is done. Aurelius provides a generic record Proxy<T> for lazy loading.

Let's make the User property in TPost a lazy loading property. We need to use the Proxy<TUser> record. Now, we are not able to access the TUser directly, but we need to use Proxy's properties (Value). As a last step, we need to inform the [Association] property that the relationship behaves in a *lazy* manner. The following code shows the changes in bold:

```
uses
  ...,
  Aurelius.Types.Proxy;

...

[Entity]
[Table('Post')]
[Id('FID', TIdGenerator.Guid)]
TPost = class
private
  ...
  [Association([TAssociationProp.Lazy],
  CascadeTypeAll - [TCascadeType.Remove])]
  [JoinColumn('User', [], 'ID')]
  FUser: Proxy<TUser>;
 function getUser: TUser;
 procedure setUser(const Value: TUser);
public
  ...
  property User: TUser read getUser write setUser;
end;

...

function TPost.getUser: TUser;
begin
 result := FUser.Value;
end;

procedure TPost.setUser(const Value: TUser);
begin
 FUser.Value := Value;
end;

...
```

Changes to introduce lazy loading of entities

Next, we would like to change the loading behavior of Posts in TUser entity. This time, the property is of TList type. Proxy<T> record can be used in this case as well with a small caveat; in addition to the TPost

objects, we need to manually instantiate and destroy the corresponding
TList; otherwise an access violation will be raised the moment we try to
retrieve the content of Posts. Aurelius provides some methods for this
purpose as shown in the following code:

```
[Entity]
[Table('User')]
[Id('FID', TIdGenerator.Guid)]
TUser = class
private
  ...
  [ManyValuedAssociation([TAssociationProp.Lazy],
  [TCascadeType.SaveUpdate, TCascadeType.Merge], 'FUser')]
  FPosts: Proxy<TList<TPost>>;
 function getPosts: TList<TPost>;
public
 constructor Create;
 destructor Destroy; override;
  ...
 property Posts: TList<TPost> read getPosts;
end;

...

constructor TUser.Create;
begin
 inherited;
 FPosts.SetInitialValue(TList<TPost>.Create);
end;

destructor TUser.Destroy;
begin
 FPosts.DestroyValue;
 inherited;
end;

function TUser.getPosts: TList<TPost>;
begin
 result := FPosts.Value;
end;

...
```

Changes to introduce lazy loading of lists

Changes to introduce lazy loading of lists

Object Manager (Container)

Aurelius implements the concept of the entity container by providing an Object Manager (TObjectManager). The object manager comes with all the required functionality to manipulate the underlying database. It operates on entities (objects) loaded from the database and allows the developer to save, update, and load them and perform queries in order to retrieve results. When the state of an entity changes, the object manager makes sure that the database is updated accordingly. Because the object manager holds a state of entities in memory, it is capable of managing the lifetime of the entity objects. Entities are instantiated and destroyed by the object manager automatically.

The object manager is designed to provide a lightweight buffer between developer and the database in use. It is meant to be a short-lived object. Very often, this point confuses newcomers to Aurelius. You instantiate an object manager every time you want to do a specific database-related operation like finding records or retrieving records under specific criteria. Once this operation is completed, the object manager should be destroyed. This means that keeping an object manager alive for the lifetime of an application is not a good use of the manager architecture and capabilities.

Typically, object manager objects are treated in try-except or try-finally blocks because the manager hits the database, and this may result to errors due to corrupted files, unavailable database servers, or other unpredictable factors.

```
uses
  ...,
  Aurelius.Engine.ObjectManager;

...

var
  ...
  objManager: TObjectManager;
begin

objManager:=TObjectManager.Create(fConnection);
  try
    ... // Entity-related operations
  finally
    objManager.Free;
  end;
  ...

end;
```

Object manager
requires an
IDBConnection
interface

This code snippet demonstrates the typical use of object managers. As you can see, we have to free the object explicitly. It is obvious that the object manager could be implemented as an interface to save the manual lifetime management, but instead it is provided as a typical class. This can be inconvenient as it generates lots of boilerplate code. In the following chapter, when we start writing code for our example application, we will see how we can do this automatically.

Criteria

The object manager provides a way to execute queries in order to retrieve results from the database. The queries are constructed by putting criteria together that represent the query you want to execute.

The simplest way to use the criteria is to take advantage of the Find<T> method in object managers. Find uses generics to determine the entity the query will return. For example, if you want to retrieve the list of posts, you can use the following code:

```
var
  ...
  postsList: TObjectList<TPost>;
begin
  objManager:=TObjectManager.Create(fConnection);
  try
    ...
    postsList:=objManager.Find<TPost>
                         .List;
    // Use postsList as a typical TObjectList
    ...
    postsList.Free; ◄─────────────────────────    Make sure you free
  finally                                          the TObjectList
    objManager.Free;
  end;
  ...
end;
```

A call to Find<TPost>.List always creates a new TObjectList even if the query itself returns nothing. You can be confident that you always have a valid instance of postsList after such call. Consequently, you need to free the instance manually; otherwise it will lead to memory leaks.

Another point to note is the type of list the object manager returns. In the preceding example, I used a TObjectList, but you can equally use a TList. There is no real difference.

The query in the code fetches all the posts from the database. This is a very basic operation, but you usually want to retrieve entities that meet some criteria. In order to achieve this, you can use Aurelius' fluent interface and provide the constraints you need. As an example, let's assume we need to retrieve all the posts that were created today. There is a number of ways to do this in Aurelius, but I find the use of Linq language extremely simple. In the following example, I use the Add method but you can also use the Where statement. They are equivalent.

```
uses
  ...,
  System.SysUtils,
  Aurelius.Criteria.Linq;

...

begin
  ...
  try
    ...
    postsList:=objManager.Find<TPost>
                      .Add(Linq['DateTime'] = Now)
                      .List;
    ...
    postsList.Free;
  finally
    ...
  end;
  ...
end;
```

As you can observe in the code, Aurelius allows the use of relational operators as part of the criteria statements. It supports a range of operations including string manipulation and the ability to directly use SQL statements. The official technical manual provides more details on this topic.

One very interesting consequence of the fluent interface is the ability to drill deep into properties of entities that represent associations. TPost holds a reference to the owner (TUser). This represents an association in ORM terms. If we want to expand the preceding query and extract the posts for which the user's name is John, we have to add the following lines:

```
...
postsList:=objManager.Find<TPost>
                    .Add(Linq['DateTime'] = Now)
            .CreateAlias('User','u')
            .Add(Linq['u.Name'] = 'John')
                    .List;
...
```

What we did is to create an alias to the property of the entity class that represents the association. We assigned the letter *u* to the property User, but this is an arbitrary choice; I can use any string for alias including the string *user*. The important point here is that we need to create an alias to get access to the properties of the associated entity. From this point onward, we can create any criteria we need and refer back to the properties of the association by using the *u.* connotation. For completion, creating aliases is not the only way to access associations; SubCriteria can also be used but I find aliases much more efficient purely because it generates clear statements in the code, and I can follow the logic of the criteria very easily. But if you prefer SubCriteria, there is no real reason not to use it.

Note   Whenever you want to access an association in an entity object, you should *always* create an alias or subcriteria. Otherwise, Aurelius will throw an error as it will try to locate a field by that name. In the following code, Aurelius will attempt to locate the User.Name field, which will lead to an error:

```
...
postsList:=objManager.Find<TPost>
                      .Add(Linq['DateTime'] = Now)
                      .Add(Linq['User.Name'] = 'John')
                      .List;

...
```

Projections

Projections are also provided by the object manager as they are basically extensions to the criteria. Generally speaking, we refer to projections when we want to retrieve specific values either directly from a list of entities or as a result of calculations and grouping. For all other cases, we refer to criteria.

We use Select to create a projection. Select can manage a list of projections via TProjections.ProjectionList, and there are a number of functions that can be used with it. Please refer to the official manual for the most up-to-date list of the functions.

Because projections are designed to retrieve values, it follows that they do not return lists of entities but rather lists of values. In Aurelius, each projection result is held in a TCriteriaResult object.

Building on our example, let's find out how many posts exist in the database.

```
uses
  ...,
  Aurelius.Criteria.Base,
  Aurelius.Criteria.Projections;

...
```

```
var
  ...
  projResults: TObjectList<TCriteriaResult>;
  projRes: TCriteriaResult;
begin
  projResults:=objManager.Find<TPost>
                         .Select(TProjections.ProjectionList
                                 .Add(TProjections.Count('ID'))
                             )
                         .ListValues;
  for projRes in projResults do
    Writeln(projRes.Values[0]);
  projResults.Free;
end;
```

In the code, I created a projection list. Because I have only one projection, this is not strictly necessary. I could have just written it in one line as follows using UniqueValue because I know that I expect only one value from the projection:

```
...
  .Select(TProjections.Count('ID')))
  .UniqueValue;
...
```

I personally prefer to create lists even when I have only one projection because it gives me a standardized way of building projections and also allows me to add another condition to the list very easily. In terms of accessing the projection results, you need to iterate through the list of TCriteriaResult in order to retrieve the desired value. Additionally, we need to manually free the instance of the result list.

A call to ListValues always creates an instance of
TObjectList<TCriteriaResult> even if the content is empty. This means
that we need to check what the list holds every time we access the content.
The following code adds the check for this situation:

```
...
for projRes in projResults do
  if projRes.Values[0] <> Null then
    Writeln(projRes.Values[0]);
...
```

In the case of UniqueValue, the call can return nil if there is no relevant
content. In this case, we need to do a separate check using Assigned.

So far, we have the total number of posts. Now, we would like to know
the number of posts per month. In order to get this, we can group the
counts of posts based on the month of the field DateTime. This is easy in
Aurelius as the code that follows shows:

```
begin
  projResults:=objManager.Find<TPost>
                .Select(TProjections.ProjectionList
              .Add(TProjections.Count('ID').As_('Num'))
              .Add(TProjections.Month('DateTime').As_('Month'))
              .Add(TProjections.Group(
                  TProjections.Month('DateTime')
                  ))
                        )
                .ListValues;
  ...
end;
```

There are two steps here. First, I add a projection to retrieve the month
of the posts using the Month projection method. Then, I group the results
based on the month component of the DateTime field of TPost.

This code will populate projResults with TCriteriaResult objects. Each TCriteriaResult will provide values for the two projections (count of posts and month of posts) we defined. I can get the values using a simple for loop.

```
...
  for projRes in projResults do
  begin
    if (projRes.Values[0] <> Null) and (projRes.Values[1] <>
    Null) then
      Writeln('Num: '+VarToStr(projRes.Values[0]) +
              ' | Month: '+VarToStr(projRes.Values[1]));
  end;
...
```

The indices correspond to the order I added the projections when I built the statement. Note that in this case, I had to use VarToStr to build the string in the Writeln statement. Many times, keeping track of the order of the projection values is not convenient especially if you need to add and remove projections during testing phases. A better and more efficient way to manage the values in TCriteriaResult is to name the values you retrieve. This can easily be done using the .As_ method as demonstrated in the preceding code. Once you assign the names, you can access them in a more readable way.

```
...
  for projRes in projResults do
  begin
    if (projRes.Values['Num'] <> Null) and
                      (projRes.Values['Month'] <> Null) then
      Writeln('Num: '+VarToStr(projRes.Values['Num']) +
              ' | Month: '+VarToStr(projRes.Values['Month']));
  end;
```

• • •

One last point about the projection code: you may notice that in order to group the result by the month of the DateTime field, I call again TProjections.Month method even after I assign the name *Month* to the same projection in the preceding two lines. Thus, it looks natural to write

• • •

```
.Add(TProjections.Group('Month'))
```

• • •

Unfortunately, this approach does not work and for good reason. The value *Month* is known to Aurelius only after the list of projections has been executed. Therefore, Aurelius cannot resolve it as part of the projection itself.

On a more general note, Aurelius provides an implementation of the Linq language. This simplifies the code in a way as it offers code that is more compact. For example, instead of writing

• • •

```
.Add(TProjections.Count('ID').As_('Num'))
.Add(TProjections.Month('DateTime').As_('Month'))
```

• • •

I could use the following statements:

• • •

```
.Add(Linq['Id'].As_('Num'))
.Add(Linq['DateTime'].Month.As_('Month'))
```

• • •

Automapping

The attributes to map a class to an entity provide great degree of flexibility to the developer when it comes to defining how Aurelius should treat the underlying tables, columns, and associations in the database. One drawback to this is that it may turn to a time-consuming process especially when the workflow of work puts the database first. For such cases, but, also, to provide simplicity of use, Aurelius introduces the [Automapping] attribute. Decorating a class with the [Entity] and [Automapping] attributes removes the need to visit every property and association in the class and provide explicit instructions about how Aurelius should treat each field and property. The automapping procedure follows a number of rules and conventions that can be found in the official documentation.

There is a small catch with automapping. When Aurelius identifies fields to map, it checks the name and if it starts with capital F (a commonly followed convention), it extracts the letter and names the table column after the remainder string. For example, if we have a field named FSurname, Aurelius will map it to the Surname column in the database table. In all other cases, Aurelius will add the F_ prefix. Thus, a field named fSurname will become F_fSurname.

If you still find the procedure of adding the [Automapping] attribute to each entity overwhelming or time-consuming in a large database schema, you can change Aurelius global behavior by changing the global configuration AutoMappingMode property to Full from the default ByClass value. Full automapping mode will automatically map any entity that is registered to Aurelius.

```
uses
  ...,
  Aurelius.Global.Config;
var
  ...,
  config: TGlobalConfigs;
```

```
begin
  ...
  config:=TGlobalConfigs.GetInstance;
  config.AutoMappingMode:=TAutomappingMode.Full;
  ...
end
```

If you want to achieve the opposite result (exclude properties and fields from automapping), you can decorate them with the [Transient] attribute.

Summary

This chapter presents TMS Aurelius. Step by step, we start by looking at the different installation options and then move to explore how ORM features as provided by the framework. This introduction sets the scene to show how Aurelius can be used in a real-life application. The next chapter presents the example application that we are going to use to put Aurelius at work.

References

Embarcadero, n.d. *Attributes (RTTI)*. [Online] Available at:
http://docwiki.embarcadero.com/RADStudio/Rio/en/Attributes_(RTTI)
[Accessed 04 03 2019].

Hodges, N., 2014. *Coding in Delphi*. s.l.:Nepeta Enterprises.

CHAPTER 3

Call Center Application

We are now ready to make our work more practical. We have seen different approaches in using ORM frameworks, and we have a good understanding of the fundamentals of Aurelius. In this chapter, we work on setting up the building blocks that will allow us to see Aurelius in practice.

The Application

For the purpose of this book, we are going to develop the back end and the code of the database layer of an application that manages data from a call center. The data set and the dashboard come from Trump Excel (Bansal, 2019). Sumit Bansal has created a great site on Excel and offers data from a call center free to use. I have modified the original data file slightly by adding some columns that are more suitable for our examples.

The call center provides support to customers of a business that has five departments (air conditioner, fridge, television, toaster, washing machine), and the center employs eight agents who handle the calls (Becky, Dan, Diane, Greg, Jim, Joe, Martha, Stewart).

© John Kouraklis 2019

J. Kouraklis, *Introducing Delphi ORM*, https://doi.org/10.1007/978-1-4842-5013-6_3

The dataset covers the operations of the center for the duration of a month (January 2016). The workflow in the center is as follows:

1. A customer calls the center. The IT system assigns a Call ID to the call and records the date (Date) and the time the call reaches the center (Queue Enter Time).

2. The call stays in a waiting queue until an agent is available. When an agent is released, the call is transferred to the Agent and the system records the time (Queue Exit Time) of transfer. At the same time, the call is flagged as Answered.

3. The agent deals with the call for as long as it is necessary (Call Duration) and records the Department that the call is relevant to.

4. At this stage, the call can be either Resolved or not.

5. In the end, the caller rates the agent in a satisfaction scale from 1 to 5 (Satisfaction Rating).

6. Sometimes, a call may be transferred to an agent, but for some reasons (technical or others) the call drops. In this case, the call is logged as both not Answered and not Resolved.

You can find the data in the CallCentreData.csv comma-separated values (CSV) file in the Misc folder. It comes with the code of this book. Figure 3-1 shows what the file looks like, and the first row shows the headers as indicated in the preceding bullet points.

	A	B	C	D	E	F	G	H	I	J
1	Call Id	Date	Queue Enter Time	Queue Exit Time	Agent	Department	Answered (Y/N)	Resolved	Call Duratic	Satisfaction Rating
2	ID0001	01/01/2016	9:12:58	9:14:47	Diane	Washing Machine	Y	Y	0:02:23	3
3	ID0002	01/01/2016	9:12:58	9:14:08	Becky	Air Conditioner	Y	N	0:04:02	3
4	ID0003	01/01/2016	9:47:31	9:47:41	Stewart	Washing Machine	Y	Y	0:02:11	3
5	ID0004	01/01/2016	9:47:31	9:48:24	Greg	Washing Machine	Y	Y	0:00:37	2
6	ID0005	01/01/2016	10:00:29	10:02:04	Becky	Toaster	Y	Y	0:01:00	3

Figure 3-1. Excerpt from the log file with the call center data set

The application has three panels: the first one holds the Dashboard, the second one the Department management, and the last one the Agent management.

Dashboard

The Dashboard page can be seen in Figure 3-2. It has a sidebar where the user can filter the results by weeks in the month, and it includes a number of panels.

- A panel with the overall satisfaction score, the total calls for the period of one month, the average answer speed (sec), the abandon rate (%), and the calls per minute

- A list with the statistics about the agents: total calls, answered calls, average speed of answer(sec), call resolution (%), and call resolution trend

- A chart with the call abandon rate by department

- A chart with the satisfaction score per agent

- A panel with the service-level agreement limits regarding the number of calls answered in less than 180 seconds and the number of calls with satisfaction score of less than 3

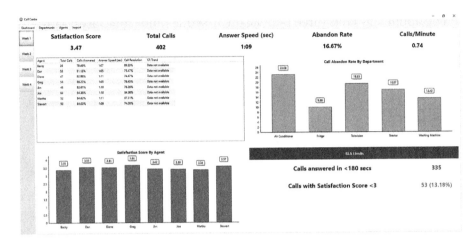

Figure 3-2. *The Dashboard tab*

Departments

Figure 3-3 shows the tab with the departments. It consists of a grid at the top with the stored departments in the database. In the grid you can, also, see the ID (primary key) for demonstration purposes. At the bottom of this grid, there are three buttons that allow the user to add, edit, and delete departments.

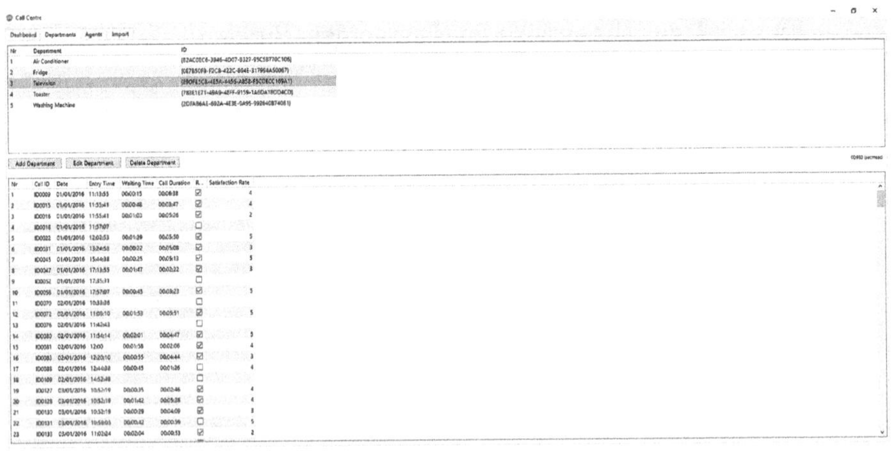

Figure 3-3. *The Departments tab*

Each one of these actions shows a window like the one in Figure 3-4. The labels and the buttons are self-explanatory.

There is another grid that fills in the rest of the form. When a department is selected in the top grid, the user can see the calls filtered by the selected department.

Figure 3-4. *The form allows the addition and editing of the departments*

Agents

The management of the agents follows the same logic as the department management (Figure 3-5). In terms of design and functionality, they remain the same.

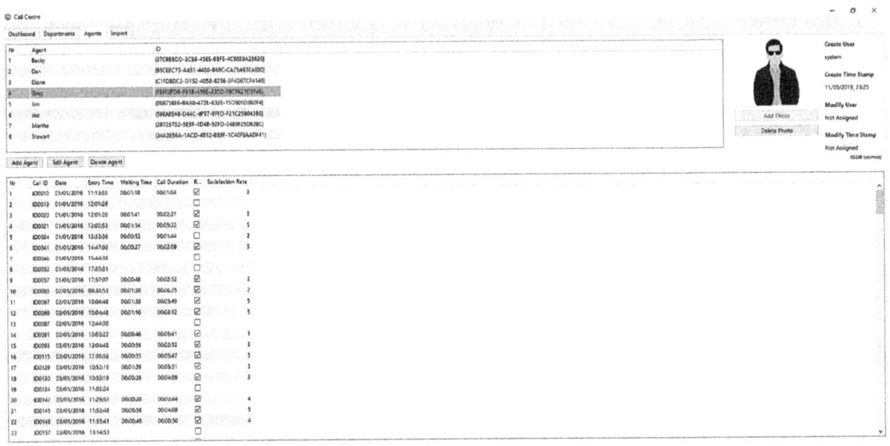

Figure 3-5. *The Agents tab*

The Interface

It's time we build our application. We start with the user interface by creating the forms we need, as in the preceding figures. The forms include a series of grids, layouts, tabs, and buttons. I am not going to go through the details of how to build the GUI because it will take unnecessary space and will distract us from the main purpose of this book. You can find a skeleton project that we will use in this and the next chapters in the code that accompanies this book. The project is named `CallCentreSkeleton`.

In order to make it easier to follow the code in the rest of the book, there are a number of points to raise regarding the design of `CallCentreSkeleton`:

- The dashboard has a sidebar that filters the data per week. We will update the data in `updateDashboard`, which is called in the `OnChange` event of the `TabControl`.

- We will add update methods for the agents and the departments in later chapters.

- There is a `setupGUI` method that initializes the GUI the first time the application runs.

The skeleton project is runnable. Open the project and just run it. In the main form (`TFormMain` in `MainForm.pas`), you can click the buttons in the sidebar, change the tabs, and click the "Add Agent" or "Add Department" buttons in the corresponding tabs. You should be able to see a separate form (`TFormEntity` in `EntityForm.pas`) in the project. We will start adding up new code shortly to the project, so you may wish to save it under a new name if you would like to keep the skeleton project intact.

Note   In our code, we will not adhere to any specific design pattern such as MVP/MVC/MVVM or any other similar approaches. Our priority is to write code that demonstrates Aurelius features rather than respect the principles of any design styles.

Entities

The model behind the call center suggests three classes: one for the departments (`TDepartment`), one for the agents (`TAgent`), and one for the calls (`TCall`). For simplicity, both `TDepartment` and `TAgent` have two simple fields:

- **ID**: A property that holds a GUID as primary key

- **Description**: A property that holds the name of the agent or the name of the department

Let's go ahead and create the entities. You can find the complete project in the folder *CallCentre – Without Database Session* in the code of the book.

1. Open the CallCentreSkeleton project or create
   a copy.

2. Add a new unit and save it under the name
   Entities.pas. This unit will hold all the attribute
   mapping of our classes.

3. In Entities.pas, add the following two classes:

```
uses
  SysUtils,
  Aurelius.Mapping.Attributes,
  Aurelius.Types.Nullable,
  Aurelius.Types.Proxy;

type
  [Entity]
  [Table('Agent')]
  [Id('FID', TIdGenerator.Guid)]
  TAgent = class
    private
      [Column('ID', [TColumnProp.Required])]
      FID: TGuid;

      [Column('Description', [TColumnProp.Required], 255)]
      FDescription: string;

      [Column('Photo', [TColumnProp.Lazy])]
      FPhoto: TBlob;
    public
      property ID: TGuid read FID write FID;
      property Description: string read FDescription write
      FDescription;
      property Photo: TBlob read FPhoto write FPhoto;
    end;
```

```
[Entity]
[Table('Department')]
[Id('FID', TIdGenerator.Guid)]
TDepartment = class
  private
    [Column('ID', [TColumnProp.Required])]
    FID: TGuid;

    [Column('Description', [TColumnProp.Required], 255)]
    FDescription: string;
public
  property ID: TGuid read FID write FID;
  property Description: string read FDescription write
  FDescription;
end;
```

I decorated the two classes with the very basic
attributes to let Aurelius know that I treat
TDepartment and TAgent as entities. I have also
indicated that FID private field works as the primary
key at the database level, uses Smart GUID engine,
and is linked to column ID. Similarly, I have
introduced the Description property to be of string
type. Then, I linked it back to the relevant field,
which I made compulsory at database level using
the TColumnProp.Required parameter and set the
length to an arbitrary value. The mapping of these
two classes is straightforward and in line with what
we discussed in Chapter 2.

4. The TCall class is more complicated as it holds more fields both compulsory and nullable; however, the principles to provide information to Aurelius are as before. In the same unit, add the following class:

```
...
type
  ...
  [Entity]
  [Table('Call')]
  [Id('FID', TIdGenerator.SmartGuid)]
  TCall = class
  private
    [Column('ID', [TColumnProp.Required])]
    FID: TGuid;

    [Column('Date', [TColumnProp.Required])]
    FDate: TDateTime;

    [Column('QueueEntryTime', [TColumnProp.Required])]
    FQueueEntryTime: TDateTime;

    [Column('QueueExitTime', [])]
    FQueueExitTime: Nullable<TDateTime>;

    [Column('ServiceStartTime', [])]
    FServiceStartTime: Nullable<TDateTime>;

    [Column('ServiceEndTime', [])]
    FServiceEndTime: Nullable<TDateTime>;

    [Column('Answered', [TColumnProp.Required])]
    FAnswered: Integer;

    [Column('Resolved', [TColumnProp.Required])]
    FResolved: Integer;
```

```
  [Column('SatisfactionRate', [])]
  FSatisfactionRate: Nullable<Integer>;

  [Column('CallID', [TColumnProp.Required], 50)]
  FCallID: string;
public
  property ID: TGuid read FID write FID;
  property Date: TDateTime read FDate write FDate;
  property QueueEntryTime: TDateTime read FQueueEntryTime
  write FQueueEntryTime;
  property QueueExitTime: Nullable<TDateTime> read
  FQueueExitTime write FQueueExitTime;
  property ServiceStartTime: Nullable<TDateTime> read
  FServiceStartTime write FServiceStartTime;
  property ServiceEndTime: Nullable<TDateTime> read
  FServiceEndTime write FServiceEndTime;
  property Answered: Integer read FAnswered write FAnswered;
  property Resolved: Integer read FResolved write FResolved;
  property SatisfactionRate: Nullable<Integer> read
  FSatisfactionRate write FSatisfactionRate;
  property CallID: string read FCallID write FCallID;
end;
```

The initial design of our application requires the
ability to indicate that a specific call is assigned to a
particular agent and refers to a specific department.
At class level, these two requirements are resolved
by introducing two properties in TCall holding a
TAgent and TDepartment classes, respectively.

```
type
  ...
  TCall = class
  private
  ...
    [Association([TAssociationProp.Lazy], CascadeTypeAll -
    [TCascadeType.Remove])]
    [JoinColumn('AgentID', [], 'ID')]
    FAgentID: Proxy<TAgent>;

    [Association([TAssociationProp.Lazy], CascadeTypeAll -
    [TCascadeType.Remove])]
    [JoinColumn('DepartmentID', [], 'ID')]
    FDepartmentID: Proxy<TDepartment>;
    function GetAgentID: TAgent;
    procedure SetAgentID(const Value: TAgent);
    function GetDepartmentID: TDepartment;
    procedure SetDepartmentID(const Value: TDepartment);
  public
    ...
    property AgentID: TAgent read GetAgentID write SetAgentID;
    property DepartmentID: TDepartment read GetDepartmentID
    write SetDepartmentID;
  end;

...
function TCall.GetAgentID: TAgent;
begin
  result := FAgentID.Value;
end;
```

```
procedure TCall.SetAgentID(const Value: TAgent);
begin
  FAgentID.Value := Value;
end;

function TCall.GetDepartmentID: TDepartment;
begin
  result := FDepartmentID.Value;
end;

procedure TCall.SetDepartmentID(const Value: TDepartment);
begin
  FDepartmentID.Value := Value;
end;
```

The corresponding private fields are where we define how Aurelius should manage them at database level. The two properties AgentID and DepartmentID are lazy loaded as the TAssociationProp.Lazy parameter is used.

The code, also, dictates what happens to the associated agent or department when a call is updated or deleted. The CascadeTypeAll - [TCascadeType.Remove] (or the equivalent CascadeTypeAllButRemove) parameter tells Aurelius that, in any other actions than removal (deletion) of a call, the department or the agent is updated. In other words, if the user deletes a call from the database, the linked agent and department records will be intact.

Lastly, the getter and setter methods for AgentID and DepartmentID are straightforward. As discussed in the previous chapter, we have to use this approach, as the corresponding fields are declared as proxies.

The preceding modifications allow us to link calls to agents and departments. It would be very convenient if we achieve the opposite as well. Given an agent (or a department), we would like to be able to drill down to all the calls they are associated with. Since Aurelius is aware of all the entities we need, we can reverse the associations by mapping properties using the ManyValuedAssociation attribute:

```
uses
  ...,
  Generics.Collections;

...
type
  ...
  TAgent = class
  private
    ...
      [ManyValuedAssociation([TAssociationProp.Lazy],
      CascadeTypeAll, 'FAgentID')]
    FCallList: Proxy<TList<TCall>>;
    function GetCallList: TList<TCall>;
  public
    ...
    constructor Create;
    destructor Destroy; override;
    property CallList: TList<TCall> read GetCallList;
  end;

  TDepartment = class
  private
    ...
```

```
      [ManyValuedAssociation([TAssociationProp.Lazy],
       CascadeTypeAll, 'FDepartmentID')]
    FCallList: Proxy<TList<TCall>>;
    function GetCallList: TList<TCall>;
  public
    ...
    constructor Create;
    destructor Destroy; override;
    property CallList: TList<TCall> read GetCallList;
  end;

...
constructor TAgent.Create;
begin
  inherited;
  FCallList.SetInitialValue(TList<TCall>.Create);
end;

destructor TAgent.Destroy;
begin
  FCallList.DestroyValue;
  inherited;
end;

function TAgent.GetCallList: TList<TCall>;
begin
  result := FCallList.Value;
end;

constructor TDepartment.Create;
begin
  inherited;
  FCallList.SetInitialValue(TList<TCall>.Create);
end;
```

```
destructor TDepartment.Destroy;
begin
  FCallList.DestroyValue;
  inherited;
end;

function TDepartment.GetCallList: TList<TCall>;
begin
  result := FCallList.Value;
end;
```

We define CallList as a typical TList<T>
property, and we pass it to Aurelius using the
ManyValuedAssociation attribute. The field defines
a lazy-loaded association which updates and merges
any changes with the associated object. Lastly, the
fields are nongeneric (TList) and proxified (Proxy);
we need to use SetInitialValue and DestroyValue
methods from Aurelius to manage their lifetime.

We need to make sure that the compiler includes all
the classes in the final binary file. This is easily done
by adding the following code in the initialization
section of Entities.pas:

```
unit Entities;

interface

...

implementation

...

initialization
  RegisterEntity(TAgent);
```

```
  RegisterEntity(TDepartment);
  RegisterEntity(TCall) ;
end.
```

Database Connection

The next step is to configure Aurelius to connect to an actual database. Based on what we discussed in Chapter 2, there are a number of ways this can be done. We will create a typical SQLite database and, since Aurelius provides a native driver to this database, we use the available connection wizard:

1. Run the wizard in *File ➤ Other... ➤ TMS Business ➤ TMS Aurelius DB Connection.*

2. In the wizard, select *Native direct connection (Driver Mode)* and *SQLite* in the Driver pop-up menu.

3. Click *Finish* and allow Aurelius to add a new Data Module in the project under the name `ConnectionModule.pas`.

4. Open the module in the design editor, right-click `AureliusConnection1` component and, in *Connection Settings*, add the `database.db` as the name of the database file. Then, close the form with the settings.

5. The `ConnectionModule` unit exposes a global variable named `SQLiteConnection` which provides reference to Aurelius connection. Although having a global variable is not considered the best way to write code, in our case it is sufficient.

6. In MainForm.pas, add the following code:

```
uses                                    This will create a new
  ...,                                  instance of the SQLite
  ConnectionModule,                     connection module
  Aurelius.Engine.DatabaseManager;

...

procedure TFormMain.FormCreate(Sender: TObject);
var
  dbManager: TDatabaseManager;
begin
  SQLiteConnection:=TSQLiteConnection.Create(self);
  dbManager:=TDatabaseManager.Create(SQLiteConnection.CreateConnection);
  try
    dbManager.UpdateDatabase;         This will update the
  finally                             schema in the database
    dbManager.Free;
  end;
  ...
end;
```

We first create an instance of the connection module. This provides access to the IDBConnection interface which is required every time we want to do operations on the database. Then, we define a local variable of TDatabaseManager which is used to update the database. You can notice that in order to create the database manager, I had to pass an instance of IDBConnection. This is supplied by the ConnectionModule as it is demonstrated in the preceding code.

In the code, I call dbManager.UpdateDatabase as the first thing that the application should do. UpdateDatabase retrieves the schema from the database and compares it with the current entity structure (virtual database objects) as defined by the mapping attributes. Then, it executes SQL statements to synchronize the database structure with the virtual database objects.

An alternative way to update the database schema is to combine the preceding code to a direct call to TDatabaseManager.Update class procedure as follows:

```
...
  SQLiteConnection:=TSQLiteConnection.Create(self);
  TDatabaseManager.Update(SQLiteConnection.CreateConnection);
...
```

Note   UpdateDatabase is not destructive. This means that if you delete some properties from an entity, Aurelius will not delete the corresponding columns in the database. This is something you need to do manually via SQL scripts.

The official manual indicates that the database manager provides another procedure that allows the creation and update of the database: BuildDatabase. This method is considered deprecated but still can be in use in code. The end result is the same as it updates the database schema as well; however, there is a slight difference. BuildDatabase does not perform reverse engineering of the database schema and any comparisons with the virtual database object; it, rather, starts executing the SQL statements based on the current state of code in the entities. If your database is really huge with hundreds of tables and columns, this approach may save you a few second which, in reality, may not even be noticeable. In any case, the recommended and modern way to update the database is to use UpdateDatabase.

IDatabaseSession

The database manager and, similarly, the object manager are declared as typical objects in Aurelius. This means that every time we use them, we naturally instantiate the objects and, eventually, we need to free them manually. This may become a source of boilerplate code especially if one considers the frequent usage of the object manager. In order to simplify this process, we will hide all those objects inside an interface (IDatabaseSession), and then we will use it as an adapter to pass the lifetime management of both objects to the interface. The code can be seen in the *CallCentre – With Database Session* folder.

1. Add a new unit in the project and save it under the name Database.Session.Types.pas.

2. Then, add the following code:

```
unit Database.Session.Types;

interface

uses
  Aurelius.Engine.DatabaseManager,
  Aurelius.Engine.ObjectManager;

type
  IDatabaseSession = interface
    ['{7CA1B4A1-F339-47EE-AE17-9436853A618E}']
    function databaseManager: TDatabaseManager;
    function objectManager: TObjectManager;
  end;

implementation

end.
```

3. Add a new unit in the project as Database. Session.pas.

4.   Add the next code snippet:

```
unit Database.Session;

interface

uses
  Database.Session.Types,
  Aurelius.Engine.DatabaseManager,
  Aurelius.Drivers.Interfaces,
  Aurelius.Engine.ObjectManager;

type
  TDatabaseSession = class (TInterfacedObject, IDatabaseSession)
  private
    fConnection: IDBConnection;
    fDatabaseManager: TDatabaseManager;
    fObjectManager: TObjectManager;
  public
    constructor Create(const aConnection: IDBConnection);
    destructor Destroy; override;
{$REGION 'Interface'}
    function databaseManager: TDatabaseManager;
    function objectManager: TObjectManager;
{$ENDREGION}
  end;

implementation

constructor TDatabaseSession.Create(const aConnection:
IDBConnection);
begin
  Assert(aConnection <> nil);
```

```
  inherited Create;
  fConnection:=aConnection;
end;

function TDatabaseSession.databaseManager: TDatabaseManager;
begin
  if not Assigned(fDatabaseManager) then
    fDatabaseManager:=TDatabaseManager.Create(fConnection);
  Result:=fDatabaseManager;
end;

destructor TDatabaseSession.Destroy;
begin
  fDatabaseManager.Free;
  fObjectManager.Free;
  inherited;
end;

function TDatabaseSession.objectManager: TObjectManager;
begin
  if not Assigned(fObjectManager) then
    fObjectManager:=TObjectManager.Create(fConnection);
  Result:=fObjectManager;
end;

end.
```

There are a number of things happening in this unit.
First, in Create, we check if the passed IDBConnection
is valid. This is not relevant to Aurelius, but it is good
practice to always check the injected parameters. Then,
we store the connection for future use. The functions
that return both the database manager and the object
manager check if there is already a valid instance of the

relative manager stored in the object. If this is the case, then they return the instance; otherwise, they create a new one.

5. In MainForm.pas, under the FormCreate event, we can now use the IDatabaseSession interface:

```
uses
  ...,
  Database.Session.Types,
  Database.Session;

...

procedure TFormMain.FormCreate(Sender: TObject);
var
  dbSession: IDatabaseSession;
begin
  SQLiteConnection:=TSQLiteConnection.Create(self);
  dbSession:=TDatabaseSession.Create(SQLiteConnection.
  CreateConnection);
  dbSession.databaseManager.UpdateDatabase;
  setupGUI;
end;
```

This looks simpler and more efficient. We still need to pass the IDBConnection to the constructor, and then we get access to the database manager and the object manager via the functions as exposed by the interface. In this instance, we do not need to free the objects.

If you are looking for more complete code, a try-except branch should wrap the call to UpdateDatabase, but I do not include it in this code and in the following examples purely for simplicity.

Summary

In this chapter, we set up the background to explore Aurelius further. The example application is introduced (`CallCentre`), and we defined the entities and the database connection as per our design and requirements. Furthermore, the `IDatabaseSession` interface is developed. In the next chapter, we will start using this interface by executing simple tasks.

Reference

Bansal, S., 2019. *Trump Excel*. [Online] Available at: `https://trumpexcel.com/call-center-performance-dashboard-excel/` [Accessed 01 04 2019].

CHAPTER 4

Basic Operations

The `CallCentre` application is in a state where it provides the necessary GUI interaction to allow us to explore Aurelius' features. In this chapter, we investigate how we can manage basic database operations and, near the end, we deal with managing a big number of transactions. The initial project to start with is in the *CallCentre – Without Utilities* folder.

Adding Entities

We have two entities to manage in our application: agents and departments. Adding them is pretty straightforward.

1. Go to `MainForm.pas`, in the `OnClick` event of `btAddDepartment` button.

2. Add the following code:

```
uses
  ...,
  Database.Session.Types,
  Database.Session,
  Entities;
...
```

```
procedure TFormMain.btAddDepartmentClick
(Sender: TObject);
var
  ...
  session: IDatabaseSession;
  department: TDepartment;
begin
  ...

  if form.ShowModal = mrOk then
  begin
    session:=TDatabaseSession.Create(SQLiteConnection.
    CreateConnection);
    department:=TDepartment.Create;
    department.Description:=Trim(form.edEntity.Text);

    try
      session.objectManager.Save(department);
    except
      if not session.objectManager.IsAttached
      (department) then
        department.Free;
    end;

    // Here we need to update the list of departments
    in the form
  end;
  ...
end;
```

3. Then, switch to the OnClick event of btAddAgent
   button and add similar code to manage TAgent.

```
procedure TFormMain.btAddAgentClick(Sender: TObject);
var
  ...
  session: IDatabaseSession;
  agent: TAgent;
begin
  ...

  if form.ShowModal = mrOk then
  begin
    session:=TDatabaseSession.Create(SQLiteConnection.
    CreateConnection);
    agent:=TAgent.Create;
    agent.Description:=Trim(form.edEntity.Text);

    try
      session.objectManager.Save(agent);
    except
      if not session.objectManager.IsAttached(agent)
      then
        agent.Free;
    end;

    // Here we need to update the list of agents in the
    form
  end;
  ...
end;
```

We declare two variables: one for the database session (IDatabaseSession) and one for the relevant entity (TDepartment/TAgent). Remember, we use the IDatabaseSession interface to get access to the object manager. We pass an IDBConnection to the database session constructor as retrieved by the connection module, and we normally create an instance of the entity.

Then, we call Save, a method provided by the object manager to convert our object to a persistent one in the database. Initially, when we create a new instance of an entity, the ID field that represents the primary key in the database has the default value (0 if it is an integer or an empty GUID in our case).

Once the object is saved, this field is populated with the actual primary key. Additionally, the object manager is now aware of the existence of this entity in both the physical and virtual databases, and it is able to manage the lifetime of the object by making sure that the instance is eventually freed. Now, it works as the owner of the object.

However, in the case where something unpredictable happens while the object manager is attempting to save the entity (e.g., bad I/O operation, damaged network, or physical medium), an exception is generated. At this stage, the object manager might not have the chance to get ownership of the object depending on when the exception occurs. Consequently, the object may not be freed by the object manager. We need to do this in code. The code in the except part of the try-except structure demonstrates exactly this step; using IsAttached, we check if the object manager owns the object. If not, we free it manually.

Listing Entities

Before we continue adding more entity operations in our code, it is better if you are able to see the stored entries. We are going to add code to retrieve the stored entries from our database.

1. In MainForm.pas, add two new procedures in the private section of TFormMain named updateDepartments and updateAgents.

2. Add the following code in the method:

```
type
  ...
  TFormMain = class(TForm)
  ...
  private
    ...
    procedure updateDepartments;
    procedure updateAgents;
  public
    ...
  end;

...


procedure TFormMain.updateDepartments;
var
  session: IDatabaseSession;
  departmentList: TList<TDepartment>;
  department: TDepartment;
begin
  sgDepartments.RowCount:=0;
  sgDepartmentDetails.RowCount:=0;

  session:=TDatabaseSession.Create(SQLiteConnection.
  CreateConnection);
  departmentList:=session.ObjectManager.Find<TDepartment>
              .OrderBy('Description')
              .List;

  // A safer approach is to enclose the following lines in
  // BeginUpdate/EndUpdate and try/finally blocks
  // But we will keep things simple here
```

```
  for department in departmentList do
  begin
    sgDepartments.RowCount := sgDepartments.RowCount + 1;
    sgDepartments.Cells[0, sgDepartments.RowCount - 1]:=
    sgDepartments.RowCount.ToString;
    sgDepartments.Cells[1, sgDepartments.RowCount - 1]:=
    department.Description;
    sgDepartments.Cells[2, sgDepartments.RowCount - 1]:=
    GUIDToString(department.ID);
  end;

  departmentList.Free;

  btEditDepartment.Enabled:= sgDepartments.Selected>-1;
  btDeleteDepartment.Enabled:= sgDepartments.Selected>-1;
  lbDepartmentDetailsNoEntries.Visible:=sgDepartment
  Details.RowCount = 0;
end;

...

procedure TFormMain.updateAgents;
var
  session: IDatabaseSession;
  agentList: TList<TAgent>;
  agent: TAgent;
begin
  sgAgents.RowCount:=0;
  sgAgentDetails.RowCount:=0;
```

```
session:=TDatabaseSession.Create(SQLiteConnection.
CreateConnection);
agentList:=session.ObjectManager.Find<TAgent>
             .OrderBy('Description')
             .List;
for agent in agentList do
begin
  sgAgents.RowCount := sgAgents.RowCount + 1;
  sgAgents.Cells[0, sgAgents.RowCount - 1]:=
  sgAgents.RowCount.ToString;
  sgAgents.Cells[1, sgAgents.RowCount - 1]:= agent.
  Description;
  sgAgents.Cells[2, sgAgents.RowCount - 1]:=
  GUIDToString
  (agent.ID);
end;

agentList.Free;

btEditAgent.Enabled:= sgAgents.Selected>-1;
btDeleteAgent.Enabled:= sgAgents.Selected>-1;
lbAgentDetailsNoEntries.Visible:=sgAgentDetails.
RowCount = 0;
end;
```

In the code, we retrieve the list of entities without
any filtering. For this, we need again an instance
of the object manager, which we create as we have
done before. We then use the Find<T> method
to retrieve the entities and we order them by
Description. As you can see in the code snippet,
Aurelius' fluent interface allows us to concatenate

methods (actions) in a way that generates a very readable line of code. Eventually, the object manager returns a list object of the entities.

It is worth mentioning that the object manager is able to manage the lifetime of the entities in the list. The list itself (`departmentList`/`agentList`) needs to be freed explicitly. We are able to access the entities in the list by simply iterating through the list the usual way (`for` loop), and we access the properties of the entities directly as we declared them non-null in the class. As we will see later on, nullable properties are treated slightly differently.

The approach we used is very typical. We created the list, iterated through the items, and destroyed it. Aurelius offers an alternative and more convenient way to achieve the same result by implementing database cursors. Cursors are interfaced objects; therefore, the need to manually free is not present. Moreover, we do not need to declare the `agentList` at all.

```
...
for agent in .Find<TAgent>
             .OrderBy('Description')
             .Open do
begin
  // Populate the grid
end;
...
```

3. We now need to use the preceding methods in
    the appropriate places (when the user adds a new
    department or agents and when the user changes
    the tab to the departments and agents).

```
...
procedure TFormMain.btAddDepartmentClick
(Sender: TObject);
...
begin
  ...
  if form.ShowModal = mrOk then
  begin
    ...
    try
      ...
    except
      ...
    end;

    updateDepartments;

  end;
  ...
end;

procedure TFormMain.btAddAgentClick(Sender: TObject);
...
begin
  ...
  if form.ShowModal = mrOk then
  begin
    ...
```

```
        try
          ...
        except
          ...
        end;

      updateAgents;

    end;
    ...
  end;

  procedure TFormMain.TabControl1Change(Sender: TObject);
  begin
    ...
    if TabControl1.ActiveTab = tiAgents then
      updateAgents;
    if TabControl1.ActiveTab = tiDepartments then
      updateDepartments;
  end;
```

Editing (Updating) Entities

The editing of an entity requires three steps:

- To retrieve the entity in the object manager

- To make changes to the properties of the entity

- To update the entity in the database

Go to the OnClick events of btEditDepartment and btEditAgent buttons and add the following code:

```
procedure TFormMain.btEditDepartmentClick(Sender: TObject);
var
  form: TFormEntity;
  session: IDatabaseSession;
  department: TDepartment;
begin
  session:=TDatabaseSession.Create(SQLiteConnection.CreateConnection);
  department:=session.objectManager.Find<TDepartment>(StringToGUID(
                                    sgDepartments.Cells[2,
sgDepartments.Selected]));
  if Assigned(department) then
  begin
    form:=TFormEntity.Create(self);
    form.lbTitle.Text:='Edit Department';
    form.Caption:='Edit Department';
    form.btAction.Text:='Update';
    form.lbEntity.Text:='Department';


    form.edCode.Text:=GUIDToString(department.ID);
    form.edEntity.Text:=department.Description;


    if form.ShowModal = mrOk then
    begin
      department.Description:=Trim(form.edEntity.Text);
      session.objectManager.Flush(department);
      updateDepartments;

  end;

    form.Free;
  end;
end;


procedure TFormMain.btEditAgentClick(Sender: TObject);
var
  form: TFormEntity;
  session: IDatabaseSession;
  agent: TAgent;
begin
  session:=TDatabaseSession.Create(SQLiteConnection.CreateConnection);
  agent:=session.objectManager.Find<TAgent>(StringToGUID(
                                    sgAgents.Cells[2,
```

If you are using the
CallCentreSkeleton project,
replace the original assignments

103

```
sgAgents.Selected]));
  if Assigned(agent) then
  begin
    form:=TFormEntity.Create(self);
    form.lbTitle.Text:='Edit Agent';
    form.Caption:='Edit Agent';
    form.btAction.Text:='Update';
    form.lbEntity.Text:='Agent';

    form.edCode.Text:=GUIDToString(agent.ID);
    form.edEntity.Text:=agent.Description;

    if form.ShowModal = mrOk then
    begin
      agent.Description:=Trim(form.edEntity.Text);
      session.objectManager.Flush(agent);
      updateAgents;
    end;

    form.Free;
  end;

end;
```

If you are using the CallCentreSkeleton project, replace the original assignments

We use the object manager's Find to retrieve the entity from the database in the same way we used it when we retrieved the full list. The difference now is that we need only one specific entity. Thus, we supply the ID (primary key) with the call to the Find method. Naturally, the query will now return a single entity which is managed by the object manager. Thus, there is no need to free it explicitly.

In the case where the object manager cannot find the specific entity, the object will be nil. This should not happen if you have one user accessing the database, but in multi-user environments, other users may delete entries from the database while our code is trying to acquire them. Thus, it is good idea to check against this using the Assign method as in the code.

Finally, we instruct Aurelius to push the changes back to the database by calling Flush. Note that we pass the object to Flush as we know exactly which entity instance has been modified.

Looking back at the code we have written so far, one can observe that there is a lot of repetition. When we add and edit departments and agents, we essentially write the same code by calling Save or Flush.

We can consolidate much of it by using SaveOrUpdate method and the very useful generics. SaveOrUpdate checks if the entity's ID property has a value other than the default. If so, the object manager saves the entity; otherwise it updates it. We are going to create a helper class that uses this method:

1. Add a new unit in the project and save it as
    Database.Utilities.pas.

2. Add the following code in this unit:

    ```
    unit Database.Utilities;

    interface

    uses
      Aurelius.Engine.ObjectManager;

    type
      TDatabaseUtilities<T: class> = class
        class procedure edit(const aObjManager:
        TObjectManager; const aEntity: T);
      end;

    implementation

    uses
      Aurelius.Mapping.Attributes;

    { TDatabaseUtilities<T> }

    class procedure TDatabaseUtilities<T>.edit(const
    aObjManager: TObjectManager; const aEntity: T);
    ```

```
begin
  Assert(aObjManager <> nil);
  Assert(aEntity <> nil);

  try
    aObjManager.SaveOrUpdate(aEntity);
    aObjManager.Flush(aEntity);
  except
    if not aObjManager.IsAttached(aEntity) then
        aEntity.Free;
  end;
end;

end.
```

3. In MainForm.pas and in the following procedures, replace the whole try-except part with a call to TDatabaseUtilities.edit as in the following code:

```
procedure TFormMain.btAddDepartmentClick
(Sender: TObject);
...
begin
  ...
  if form.ShowModal = mrOk then
  begin
    session:=TDatabaseSession.Create(SQLiteConnection.
    CreateConnection);
    department:=TDepartment.Create;
    department.Description:=Trim(form.edEntity.Text);

    TDatabaseUtilities<TDepartment>.edit(session.
    objectManager, department);

    updateDepartments;
```

```
  end;
  ...
end;

procedure TFormMain.btAddAgentClick(Sender: TObject);
...
begin
  ...
  if form.ShowModal = mrOk then
  begin
    session:=TDatabaseSession.Create(SQLiteConnection.
    CreateConnection);
    agent:=TAgent.Create;
    agent.Description:=Trim(form.edEntity.Text);

    TDatabaseUtilities<TAgent>.edit(session.
    objectManager, agent);

    updateAgents;

  end;
  ...
end;

procedure TFormMain.btEditDepartmentClick
(Sender: TObject);
...
begin
  ...
    if form.ShowModal = mrOk then
    begin
      department.Description:=Trim(form.edEntity.Text);
      TDatabaseUtilities<TDepartment>.edit(session.
      objectManager, department);
```

```
      updateDepartments;
    end;
  end;

  procedure TFormMain.btEditAgentClick(Sender: TObject);
  ...
  begin
    ...
    if form.ShowModal = mrOk then
    begin
      agent.Description:=Trim(form.edEntity.Text);

      TDatabaseUtilities<TAgent>.edit(session.object
      Manager, agent);

      updateAgents;
    end;
  end;
```

Managing Blobs

TAgent includes a Photo property that holds an image of the agents. In the Agents tab in the main form, at the right-hand side, there is space to show this image. At the entity level, Photo property is defined as a TBlob field. In this part, we will look at how we can manage different aspects of a blob in Aurelius.

1. When the list of the agents is updated, there is no selected row. Therefore, the image component should be empty and the add and delete photo buttons should be disabled. Go to MainForm.pas and add the following lines in updateAgents:

```
procedure TFormMain.updateAgents;
...
begin
  ...
  imPhoto.Bitmap:=nil;
  btAddPhoto.Enabled:= sgAgents.Selected>-1;
  btDeletePhoto.Enabled:= sgAgents.Selected>-1;
end;
```

2. Blobs are, basically, streams of bytes. This, consequently, means that our photos (bitmaps) will be stored as bytes and, when retrieved, the bytes should be converted back to bitmaps. In order to achieve this, we add the next two procedures in TDatabaseUtilities in Database.Utilities.pas.

```
uses
  ...,
  FMX.Graphics,
  Aurelius.Types.Blob;

interface

type
  TDatabaseUtilities<T: class> = class
    ...
    class procedure bitmapToBlob (const aBmp: TBitmap;
    const aType: string;
                                    var aBlob: TBlob);
    class procedure blobToBitmap (const aBlob: TBlob;
    var aBmp: TBitmap);
  end;
```

```
implementation

uses
  ...,
  FMX.Surfaces,
  System.Classes,
  System.SysUtils;

class procedure TDatabaseUtilities<T>.
bitmapToBlob(const aBmp: TBitmap;
  const aType: string; var aBlob: TBlob);
var
  bmp: TBitmapSurface;
  bs: TBytesStream;
begin
  bmp := TBitmapSurface.create;
  try
    bmp.assign(aBmp);
    bs := TBytesStream.create;
    try
      TBitmapCodecManager.SaveToStream(bs, bmp, aType);
      aBlob.AsBytes := bs.Bytes;
    finally
      bs.free;
    end;
  finally
    bmp.free;
  end;

end;
```

```
class procedure TDatabaseUtilities<T>.
blobToBitmap(const aBlob: TBlob;
  var aBmp: TBitmap);
var
  ms: TMemoryStream;
begin
  Assert(aBmp <> nil);
  ms := TMemoryStream.create;
  try
    aBlob.SaveToStream(ms);
    MS.Position := 0;
    aBmp.LoadFromStream(ms);
  finally
    ms.free;
  end;
end;
```

3. Back in TFormMain, in MainForm.pas, we introduce
    a private variable named photo. We are going to
    use this to update the TImage component in the
    Agents tab. We also need to add some code in the
    OnDestroy event of the form in order to make sure
    we destroy any instances of photo.

```
type
  TFormMain = class(TForm)
    ...
    procedure FormDestroy(Sender: TObject);
  private
    photo: TBitmap;
    ...
  end;

...
```

111

```
procedure TFormMain.FormDestroy(Sender: TObject);
begin
  FreeAndNil(photo);
end;
```

4. When the user selects a row in the agent list, the agent image is shown in the TImage component. We manage this in the new private procedure loadPhoto, which gets the GUID value of the selected agent entity as a parameter. loadPhoto is called in the OnCellClick event of the agents list.

```
type
  TFormMain = class(TForm)

    ...
  private

    ...
    procedure loadPhoto (const aGUID: string);
  end;

...

procedure TFormMain.loadPhoto(const aGUID: string);
var
  session: IDatabaseSession;
  agent: TAgent;
begin
  Assert(Trim(aGUID) <> '');
  FreeAndNil(photo);

  session:=TDatabaseSession.Create(SQLiteConnection.
  CreateConnection);
  agent:=session.objectManager.Find<TAgent>(Trim(aGUID));
```

```
  if Assigned(agent) and (not agent.Photo.IsNull) then
  begin
    photo:=TBitmap.Create;
    TDatabaseUtilities<TAgent>.blobToBitmap(agent.
    Photo, photo);
  end;

  imPhoto.Bitmap:=photo;
  btAddPhoto.Enabled:= not Assigned(photo);
  btDeletePhoto.Enabled:= Assigned(photo);
end;

...


procedure TFormMain.sgAgentsCellClick(const Column:
TColumn; const Row:
    Integer);
begin
  ...
  loadPhoto(sgAgents.Cells[2, sgAgents.Selected]);
end;
```

The procedure retrieves the agent from the database
and checks if the Photo property has any content
by using Aurelius' IsNull function. If content is
detected, blobToBitmap is used to load the blob
content to photo. Lastly, the GUI is being taken care
of by enabling the appropriate buttons.

5. Add a TOpenDialog component in the form and modify the OnClick event of btAddPhoto button.

```
uses
  ...,
  Aurelius.Types.Blob;

...

procedure TFormMain.btAddPhotoClick(Sender: TObject);
var
  session: IDatabaseSession;
  agent: TAgent;
  blob: TBlob;
begin
  OpenDialog1.Filter:='PNG image files|*.png';
  if OpenDialog1.Execute then
  begin
    session:=TDatabaseSession.Create(SQLiteConnection.
    CreateConnection);
    agent:=session.objectManager.Find<TAgent>(StringTo
    GUID(sgAgents.Cells[2,sgAgents.Selected]));
    if Assigned(agent) then
    begin
      imPhoto.Bitmap.LoadFromFile(OpenDialog1.FileName);
      TDatabaseUtilities<TAgent>.bitmapToBlob
      (imPhoto.Bitmap, 'png', blob);
      agent.Photo:=blob;
      TDatabaseUtilities<TAgent>.edit(session.object
      Manager, agent);
    end;
  end;
end;
```

When the user selects a PNG file, the code loads the selected agent as before. Then, the image file is passed to the TImage component, and bitmapToBlob is called to convert the bitmap to blob. Then, the entity instance is updated and, eventually, saved in the database. In the files that come with the book, you can find avatars to try it yourself in the *Misc* folder.

You may wonder why we do not pass directly the agent.Photo to bitmapToBlob. We need to use a local variable because the compiler recognizes agent.Photo as a constant and, therefore, it cannot be passed to an argument which is treated as a variable.

6. We have one last thing to do that involves blob – the ability to delete the photo. Click the btDeletePhoto album and just set the IsNull property of the TBlob to nil as follows:

```
procedure TFormMain.btDeletePhotoClick(Sender: TObject);
var
  session: IDatabaseSession;
  agent: TAgent;
  blob: TBlob;
begin
  session:=TDatabaseSession.Create(SQLiteConnection.
  CreateConnection);
  agent:=session.objectManager.Find<TAgent>(String
  ToGUID(sgAgents.Cells[2, sgAgents.Selected]));
```

```
      if Assigned(agent) then
      begin
        imPhoto.Bitmap:=nil;
        agent.Photo.IsNull:=True;
        TDatabaseUtilities<TAgent>.edit(session.
        objectManager, agent);
      end;
    end;
```

Deleting Entities

Deleting entities in Aurelius is straightforward once you get an instance of the object manager. As you can see in the following code, this task is a simple call to Remove:

```
procedure TFormMain.btDeleteDepartmentClick(Sender: TObject);
var
  session: IDatabaseSession;
  department: TDepartment;
begin
  ...
      case AResult of
        mrYes: begin
              session:=TDatabaseSession.Create(
                        SQLiteConnection.CreateConnection);
          department:=session.objectManager.Find<TDepartment>(
          StringToGUID(sgDepartments.Cells[2, sgDepartments.
          Selected]));
            if Assigned(department) then
            begin
```

```
            session.objectManager.Remove(department);
            updateDepartments;
          end;
            end;
        end;
      end);
end;

procedure TFormMain.btDeleteAgentClick(Sender: TObject);
var
   session: IDatabaseSession;
   agent: TAgent;
begin
   ...
      case AResult of
        mrYes: begin
            session:=TDatabaseSession.Create(
                    SQLiteConnection.CreateConnection);
           agent:=session.objectManager.Find<TAgent>(
           StringToGUID(sgAgents.Cells[2, sgDepartments.
           Selected]));
           if Assigned(agent) then
           begin
            session.objectManager.Remove(agent);
            updateAgentss;
           end;
            end;
        end;
      end);
end;
```

Importing Entities

All the code we developed earlier provides us with all the functionality we need to manage agents and departments. However, we miss the most important data in a call center: the calls. We could create buttons to manage calls in a similar way as we do with the agents and departments, but we will follow a different approach at this stage. We will import data from a csv file; this will demonstrate some additional features in Aurelius.

We need some additional elements in the forms. In the code files, open the project in *CallCentre – Import* folder to see the changes. I have added a separate tab to facilitate the import of the data. The tab item hosts a frame (TFrameImport) with a progress bar, a label, and a button. All this decoration is unnecessary for the essence of this book, but I wanted to create a decent user interface. The actual importing is done in the Database.Import.pas unit. The code includes manipulation of the GUI as well but, for simplicity, I will not reproduce it here. You can either check the file yourself or, if you write the code in a separate unit, you can safely focus on the parts presented here. The code should work in full.

Database.Import unit provides access to the importData procedure. This is where we work out the whole task. The signature of the procedure is as follows; it receives the filename of the data file, a reference to the well known by now IDBConnection, and a reference to the import frame.

```
procedure importData (const aFilename: string; const
aConnection: IDBConnection; const aImportFrame: TFrameImport);
```

In MainForm.pas, create an event for OnClick for the btImport, provide the option to the user to choose the file by using the TOpenDialog we added earlier, and simply call importData.

```
procedure TFormMain.FrameImportbtImportClick(Sender: TObject);
begin
  OpenDialog1.Filter:='CSV Files (*.csv)|*.csv';
```

```
  if OpenDialog1.Execute then
    importData(OpenDialog1.FileName, SQLiteConnection.
    CreateConnection, FrameImport);
end;
```

The procedure takes a series of steps. In the beginning, we want to make sure that the database is clean, but this is not necessary, strictly speaking. We achieve this by dumping and rebuilding the whole database scheme using the database manager (DestroyDatabase and BuildDatabase).

```
unit Database.Import;

interface

uses
  Aurelius.Drivers.Interfaces,
  ImportFrame;

procedure importData (const aFilename: string; const
aConnection: IDBConnection; const aImportFrame: TFrameImport);

implementation

uses
...

procedure importData (const aFilename: string; const aConnection:
IDBConnection; const aImportFrame: TFrameImport);
var
  session: IDatabaseSession;
  dbManager: TDatabaseManager;
  objManager: TObjectManager;
  ...
begin
  ...
```

```
session:=TDatabaseSession.Create(aConnection);
dbManager:=session.databaseManager;
objManager:=session.objectManager;

...

dbManager.DestroyDatabase;
dbManager.BuildDatabase;

  ...
end;

end.
```

Then, we add the agents and the departments in the database. The steps are exactly the same as those we followed earlier with the assistance of TDatabaseUtilities.

Then, the code loads the calls from the csv file and generates the TCall instances. There is some manipulation of the loaded data, but we will skip them as they are not the point of the discussion here. You can, of course, see the full code in the code files.

After we prepare the TCall object, we save it in the database with a simple call to objManager.Save. There is nothing new here; we'd been doing this already. What is different with the design of our code this time is that we need to import a good number of calls (c.1,770); it's not that big if you consider professional settings, but it is big enough to consume unnecessary resources even in a small-scale application.

The solution to this is to approach the case in a SQL-transactional way; we enter in a state where any changes to the database are done in isolation, with the assurance that the changes are successful and the database state is preserved in case of exceptions or errors. If an error occurs, the database is able to roll back to the latest stable state. In Aurelius, we can achieve this by using the IDBTransaction interface. The following code shows how the BeginTransaction, Commit, and Rollback procedures from

IDBTransaction can be used. Please note that the following code is not as the one you will find in the code file as it hides the parts that handle the user interface:

```
procedure importData (const aFilename: string; const aConnection:
IDBConnection; const aImportFrame: TFrameImport);
var
  ...,
  transaction: IDBTransaction;
begin
  ...
  transaction:=objManager.Connection.BeginTransaction
  try
    ...
    for item in list do
    begin
      ...
      call:=TCall.Create;
      ...
      objManager.Save(call);
    end;
    transaction.Commit;
  except
    transaction.Rollback;
  end;
  ...
end;
```

We set the object manager in a transactional state by calling BeginTransaction. The for-loop iterates through the lines from the data set. Each item has all the necessary information about a recorded call. We use this to generate a new TCall object and Save it in the cache of the object manager.

Eventually, and outside the `for-loop`, a call to `Commit` makes the changes persistent. You may wonder why we really need a `Commit` action when we have the `Flush` action which is also provided by the object manager. I can see two aspects in this argument which are linked:

- A call to `Flush` is, in fact, a managed call to `Commit`. `Flush` wraps the whole `try-except` code we wrote in our example.

```
...
transaction:=objManager.Connection.BeginTransaction
try
  ...
  objManager.Save(...);

  transaction.Commit;
except
  transaction.Rollback;
end;
...
```

Flush

- Following the preceding point, `Flush` appears suitable for a relatively small number of transactions. If you want to handle a good number of them, you may wish to get more control over the whole process as resources can be stretched and, additionally, you may need finer management of the situations where something goes wrong while Aurelius attempts to pass the changes to the database. `Rollback`, as it is demonstrated in the preceding code, is called in this case and reverts any changes delivered up to the point the error occurred. If you want to intervene at this step, the only way to do it is to set the object manager in a transactional state rather than simply call `Flush`.

Summary

As a matter of summarizing the chapter, please go ahead, run the code and import the data set from the csv file. You will then have populated tables in the database for the agents and the departments. Additionally, the database will have the calls imported and ready for use. We achieved all this by visiting the way that object manager manipulates entities and the associated operations. With all the data in place, we are ready to move to the next stage, to explore how Aurelius implements queries.

CHAPTER 5

Querying the Database

Our application is now capable of providing the basic management of the database entities. We can add, edit, and delete agents and departments, and our database is populated with a list of calls. Let us move on further and allow Aurelius to provide us with some useful information from the database.

Listings

In both Departments and Agents tabs, there is a grid at the bottom of the forms with information about the calls. You can find the code we use in this chapter in the *Call Centre – Listings* folder.

Departments

The grid shows data filtered by the Department or the Agent. In order to do this, you need to select a line in the Department or Agent grids. We begin with the Department grid. This grid has the following columns:

- **Nr**: Row number

- **CallID**: The ID of the call

- **Date**: The date of the call

© John Kouraklis 2019
J. Kouraklis, *Introducing Delphi ORM*, https://doi.org/10.1007/978-1-4842-5013-6_5

- **Entry Time**: The time the call entered the queue

- **Waiting Time**: The time the call stays in the queue

- **Duration**: The duration of the call when an agent picks it up

- **Resolved**: Indicated whether the issue in the call is resolved

- **Satisfaction Rate**: The satisfaction rate the customer gave to the agent

Some of the fields (CallID, Date, Entry Time, Resolved, Satisfaction Rate) are directly stored in our database so we can populate them very easily by just retrieving the data.

1. Add a new private procedure in the form (updateDepartmentList) where

```
interface

...

type
  TFormMain = class(TForm)
  ...
  private
  ...
    procedure updateDepartmentList;
  ...
  end;

...

implementation

...
```

2. Add the following lines in updateDepartmentList:

```
procedure TFormMain.updateDepartmentList;
var
  session: IDatabaseSession;
  callList: TObjectList<TCall>;
  call: TCall;
begin
  ...
  session:=TDatabaseSession.Create(SQLiteConnection.
  CreateConnection);

  callList:=session.objectManager.Find<TCall>
                          .CreateAlias('DepartmentID',
                          'department')
                            .Where(Linq['department.ID'] =
                              sgDepartments.Cells[2,
                              sgDepartments.Selected])
                          .List;
  ...
  for call in callList do
  begin
    sgDepartmentDetails.RowCount := sgDepartmentDetails.
    RowCount + 1;
    sgDepartmentDetails.Cells[0, sgDepartmentDetails.
    RowCount - 1]:= sgDepartmentDetails.RowCount.ToString;
    sgDepartmentDetails.Cells[1, sgDepartmentDetails.
    RowCount - 1]:= call.CallID;
    sgDepartmentDetails.Cells[2, sgDepartmentDetails.
    RowCount - 1]:= FormatDateTime('dd/mm/yyyy', call.Date);
```

```
sgDepartmentDetails.Cells[3, sgDepartmentDetails.
RowCount - 1]:= FormatDateTime('hh:mm:ss', call.
QueueEntryTime);

if call.Resolved = 0 then
  sgDepartmentDetails.Cells[6, sgDepartmentDetails.
  RowCount - 1]:= 'N'
else
  sgDepartmentDetails.Cells[6, sgDepartmentDetails.
  RowCount - 1]:= 'Y';

if call.SatisfactionScore.HasValue then
  sgDepartmentDetails.Cells[7, sgDepartmentDetails.
  RowCount - 1]:= call.SatisfactionScore.Value.ToString;
  end;
...
callList.Free;
...
end;
```

Nothing new here in terms of Aurelius' functionality. We retrieve the list of the calls based on the Department.ID from the first grid. Note that SatisfactionScore is a nullable field and, therefore, we check if there is a value in the field. If so, we use the Value property to TNullable<TCall> to extract the field.

The other columns of the grid require some calculations but this is straightforward. We check if nullable fields have values and we proceed with some calculations.

```
procedure TFormMain.updateDepartmentList;
var
  session: IDatabaseSession;
  callList: TObjectList<TCall>;
  call: TCall;
begin
  ...
  for call in callList do
  begin
    if call.QueueExitTime.HasValue then
      sgDepartmentDetails.Cells[4, sgDepartmentDetails.
      RowCount - 1]:=
                    FormatDateTime('hh:mm:ss', call.
                    QueueExitTime.Value - call.
                    QueueEntryTime);

    if call.ServiceStartTime.HasValue and call.ServiceEndTime.
    HasValue then
      sgDepartmentDetails.Cells[5, sgDepartmentDetails.
      RowCount - 1]:=
                    FormatDateTime('hh:mm:ss', call.
                    ServiceEndTime.Value - call.
                    ServiceStartTime.Value);
  end;
  ...
end;
```

3. Call updateDepartmentList in the OnSelectCell event of the grid with the departments:

```
procedure TFormMain.sgDepartmentsSelectCell(Sender: TObject;
const ACol, ARow:
    Integer; var CanSelect: Boolean);
```

```
begin
  ...
  updateDepartmentList;
end;
```

Agents

The grid with the details of the agents can be filled in in a similar way, but we will follow a different approach this time. When we discussed the ORM fundamentals, we saw that when entities are associated the endpoints are reciprocal. This means that you can start from one entity and reach the other directly via the association. In our case, a call is linked to an agent and, by association, if we start from the TAgent entity we should be able to get the linked TCalls which, by definition, generates a one-to-many association.

1. In Entities.pas, we have already added a TList property (CallList) in TAgent class (see Chapter 3).

2. In MainForm.pas, add a new private procedure updateAgentList to update the grid with the calls per agent:

```
interface

...

type
  TFormMain = class(TForm)
  ...
  private
  ...
    procedure updateAgentList;
  ...
  end;
```

...

implementation

...

3. Add the following lines in updateAgentList:

```
procedure TFormMain.updateAgentList;
var
  session: IDatabaseSession;
  agent: TAgent;
  call: TCall;
begin
  ...
  session:=TDatabaseSession.Create(SQLiteConnection.
CreateConnection);

  try
    agent:=session.objectManager.Find<TAgent>(
                        StringToGUID(sgAgents.Cells[2,
                        sgAgents.Selected]));

    if Assigned(agent) then
    begin
      ...

      for call in agent.CallList do
      begin
        sgAgentDetails.RowCount := sgAgentDetails.RowCount + 1;
        sgAgentDetails.Cells[0, sgAgentDetails.RowCount - 1]:=
        sgAgentDetails.RowCount.ToString;
        sgAgentDetails.Cells[1, sgAgentDetails.RowCount - 1]:=
        call.CallID;
        sgAgentDetails.Cells[2, sgAgentDetails.RowCount - 1]:=
```

```
                                        FormatDateTime
                                        ('dd/mm/yyyy',
                                        call.Date);
    sgAgentDetails.Cells[3, sgAgentDetails.RowCount - 1]:=
                                        FormatDateTime
                                        ('hh:mm:ss', call.
                                        QueueEntryTime);
    if call.QueueExitTime.HasValue then
      sgAgentDetails.Cells[4, sgAgentDetails.RowCount - 1]:=
                      FormatDateTime('hh:mm:ss', call.
                      QueueExitTime.Value - call.
                      QueueEntryTime);

    if call.ServiceStartTime.HasValue and call.
    ServiceEndTime.HasValue then
      sgAgentDetails.Cells[5, sgAgentDetails.RowCount - 1]:=
                      FormatDateTime('hh:mm:ss', call.
                      ServiceEndTime.Value - call.
                      ServiceStartTime.Value);

    if call.Resolved = 0 then
      sgAgentDetails.Cells[6, sgAgentDetails.
      RowCount - 1]:= 'N'
    else
      sgAgentDetails.Cells[6, sgAgentDetails.
      RowCount - 1]:= 'Y';

    if call.SatisfactionScore.HasValue then
      sgAgentDetails.Cells[7, sgAgentDetails.RowCount - 1]:=
                              call.SatisfactionScore.
                              Value.ToString;
    end;
  end;
```

```
finally
    sgAgentDetails.EndUpdate;
    ...
  end;
  ...
end;
```

4. Call updateAgentList in the OnSelectCell event of the agents' grid:

```
procedure TFormMain.sgAgentsSelectCell(Sender: TObject; const
ACol, ARow:
    Integer; var CanSelect: Boolean);
begin
  ...
  updateAgentList;
end;
```

In this approach, we first load the agent based on the GUID that is selected when the user clicks the agent grid, and then we iterate through agent.CallList to get the calls associated to the particular agent. The rest of the code that populates the details of the calls in the grid is exactly the same as before.

In our application, the two approaches we used bring the same result. The code that uses the CallList is much simpler. The downside of this approach is that we cannot filter the results using Aurelius features as in the first approach. Instead, we need to run through the items of the TList and cut out whatever is not desirable. This may not pose a significant matter in CallCentre application but, in general, it is much preferable to do heavy tasks at the server side. Client-side processing may consume resources that can be valuable especially in mobile platforms.

Queries (Dashboard)

The dashboard holds lot of information of different nature and in different places. If you look at the data in the dashboard, you will notice that the entire data set consists of either aggregated (e.g., total calls) or calculated (e.g., calls/minute) values. In Chapter 2, we discussed that Aurelius is able to extract such values with the use of projections. The code files are located in the *Call Centre – Queries* folder.

Before we start filling the dashboard in, we need to consider the filtering we have introduced. The left sidebar allows the user to select the weeks, and it filters the data presented in the dashboard. We are going to use this filter in every calculation we make.

For this part, we need to calculate the following metrics:

- **Average Satisfaction Score (%)**

- **Total Calls**

- **Answer Speed (min:sec)**

- **Abandon Rate (%)**

- **Calls/Minute**

- **Calls answered in less than 180 seconds**

- **Calls with satisfactory rate less than 3**

In addition to the preceding metrics, there is a list which presents data per agent (total calls, calls answered, average speed, call resolution percentage, and the call resolution trend; that is whether the agent's ability to resolve calls is improving or not or remains the same). The dashboard also holds two graphs, but we are going to deal with them in the next chapter.

Go to `MainForm.pas` and add a new private procedure called `calculateStatistics`. We need to know the week the user selected in the sidebar, so we pass this information as a parameter to the procedure:

```
interface

...

type
  ...
  TFormMain = class(TForm)
     ...
  private
    ...
    procedure calculateStatistics(const aWeek: TWeeks);
  public
    ...
  end;

...

implementation

...

procedure TFormMain.calculateStatistics(const aWeek: TWeeks);
var
  session: IDatabaseSession;
begin
  session:=TDatabaseSession.Create(SQLiteConnection.
  CreateConnection);
end;
```

For now, the only thing we do is to create a new database session, as we have done many times already. To complete the setup of this procedure, add a call in the updateDashboard procedure. This will make sure the dashboard is updated every time the user selects the tab.

```
procedure TFormMain.updateDashboard(const aWeek: TWeeks);
begin
  ...
  calculateStatistics (aWeek);
end;
```

Next, we calculate the indicators separately to demonstrate the use of different functions Aurelius offers. Many instances of the following code can be combined in one call to Aurelius as they are under the same conditions.

Average Satisfaction Score (%)

This is the average satisfaction score of the calls. If you look at the initial csv file or the database, there are calls without satisfaction score; the field is null. We should not include them in the calculation of the average score.

```
procedure TFormMain.calculateStatistics(const aWeek: TWeeks);
var
  ...
  projRes: TCriteriaResult;
begin
  ...
  projRes:=session.objectManager.Find<TCall>
                        .Select(TProjections.
                        ProjectionList
                        .Add(TProjections.
                        Avg('SatisfactionScore')
                            .As_('SatisfactionScore'))
                        )
                        .Where(not
                        Linq['SatisfactionScore'].IsNull)
                        .UniqueValue;
```

```
if projRes.Values['SatisfactionScore'] <> Null then
  lbSatisfactionValue.Text:=
             format('%2.2f', [Double(projRes.Values
             ['SatisfactionScore'])]);
else
  lbSatisfactionValue.Text:='0.00';
projRes.Free;
end;
```

Because we are retrieving one and only one result from the projection (SatisfactionScore), we get a TCriteriaResult instead of a TObjectList<TCriteriaResult>, as shown in Chapter 2. We do this by using UniqueValue. In this case, we also use the Avg function from Aurelius toolbox, and we pass a boolean expression in the Where clause to run the calculation only on valid records.

Weeks

The preceding code snippet calculates the average satisfaction score for all the calls in the database. We need to make use of the aWeek parameter in calculateStatistics. We have already inserted in the database the week of each call when we imported the data from the csv file. The value is held in the Week property of the TCall entity.

We can add a simple Linq expression to accommodate the user's choice.

```
...
projRes:=session.objectManager.Find<TCall>
                           .Select(TProjections.
                           ProjectionList
                           .Add(TProjections.
                           Avg('SatisfactionScore')
```

```
        .As_('SatisfactionScore'))
                                    )
                    .Add(Linq['Week'] = integer(aWeek)+1)
                        .Where(not
                        Linq['SatisfactionScore'].IsNull)
                .UniqueValue;
```

...

You can click the buttons in the sidebar, and the satisfaction score is calculated for each week. However, if you look at the data in the database, you will notice that there are entries with week number 5. We calculated the week for each call using the WeekOfTheMonth function. Our data refers to January 2016, a month for which the first and last days fall in the middle of weeks. Therefore, the function, correctly, returns the calendar week number.

As a result, the code we added earlier misses some calls. It uses the TWeeks identifier to select the calls, but TWeeks has only four elements. This means that the calls that appear in week 5 do not make it in the result. We will add them in week 4's calls, but we cannot do this inside the projection as we need to write some programming logic. Instead, we will create a separate function called filter and we will break the projection down. Projections in Aurelius are built using the TCriteria class as shown in the following code:

```
interface

...

type
  ...
  TFormMain = class(TForm)
    ...
  private
```

```
  ...
  function filter(const aWeek: TWeeks; const aCriteria:
  TCriteria): TCriteria;
public
  ...
end;

...

implementation

...

function TFormMain.filter(const aWeek: TWeeks; const aCriteria:
TCriteria):
    TCriteria;
begin
  if aWeek = wWeek4   then
    result:= aCriteria.Add(Linq['Week'] >= 4)
  else
    result:= aCriteria.Add(Linq['Week'] = integer(aWeek)+1);
end;

procedure TFormMain.calculateStatistics(const aWeek: TWeeks);
var
  ...
  criteria: TCriteria;
begin
  session:=TDatabaseSession.Create(SQLiteConnection.
  CreateConnection);

  criteria:=session.objectManager.Find<TCall>
                            .Select(TProjections.
                            ProjectionList
```

```
                              .Add(TProjections.
                              Avg('SatisfactionScore')
                                   .As_('SatisfactionScore'))
                               )
                              .Where(
                                   not
                                   Linq['SatisfactionScore'].
                                   IsNull);

  criteria:=filter(aWeek, criteria);

  projRes:=criteria.UniqueValue;

  ...
  lbSatisfactionValue.Text:=format('%2.2f',  [Double(projRes.
  Values['SatisfactionScore'])]);

  ...
  projRes.Free;
end;
```

We define a TCriteria variable and we build the projection without passing it to the object manager because we need to populate it with the right filter. filter function accomplishes this, and then we call UniqueValue to retrieve the required information. For simplicity, the preceding code does not include the check for null content.

In this approach, we chose to make filter return TCriteria to modify the query. Another approach would be to make filter return TLinqExpression. This would allow us to use filter, directly, in the fluent interface as we build our query. You can see this in the following code and, as you can notice, there is no need to declare criteria at all:

```
  ...
  function filter(const aWeek: TWeeks): TLinqExpression;
begin
```

```
  if aWeek = wWeek4  then
    result:= Linq['Week'] >= 4
  else
    result:= Linq['Week'] = integer(aWeek)+1;
end;
...
procedure TFormMain.calculateStatistics(const aWeek: TWeeks);
...
begin
  ...

  projRes:=session.objectManager.Find<TCall>
                           .Select(TProjections.
                           ProjectionList
                           .Add(TProjections.
                           Avg('SatisfactionScore')
                                .As_('SatisfactionScore'))
                            )
                           .Where(
                               not
                               Linq['SatisfactionScore'].
                               IsNull)
                           .Add(filter(aWeek))
                           .UniqueValue;
  ...
end;
```

We could obviously add the lines from filter function directly in the code, but we are going to need it in more than one place in our code; therefore, a function looks for better solution. As a last note, we have to free the TCriteriaResult (projRes) but not the TCriteria (criteria). criteria is automatically destroyed when UniqueValue, List, or ListValues are called.

Total Calls

This is the number of calls the center receives. There are a couple of approaches here to get this number, but I think the simplest one is the following as we saw in a previous chapter:

```
procedure TFormMain.calculateStatistics(const aWeek: TWeeks);
var
  ...
  totalCalls: integer;
begin
  ...
  criteria:=session.objectManager.Find<TCall>
                            .Select(TProjections.
                            ProjectionList
                        .Add(TProjections.Count('ID').
                        As_('TotalCalls'))
                            );
  criteria:=filter(aWeek, criteria);
  projRes:=criteria.UniqueValue;

  ...
  totalCalls:= projRes.Values['TotalCalls'];
  lbTotalCallsValue.Text:= totalCalls.ToString;

  ...

  projRes.Free;
end;
```

This time I introduce the variable totalCalls to get the result from the projection. The only reason I do this is because we will need this value for subsequent calculations.

Answer Speed

This is the average time in minutes and seconds a call stays in the queue before being assigned to an agent or dropped for any reasons.

```
procedure TFormMain.calculateStatistics(const aWeek: TWeeks);
var
  ...
begin
  ...
  criteria:=session.objectManager.Find<TCall>
                           .Select(TProjections.
                           ProjectionList
                    .Add(TProjections.Avg(
       Linq['QueueExitTime'] - Linq['QueueEntryTime']).
       As_('AnswerSpeed'))
                              )
                           .Where(not
                           Linq['QueueExitTime'].IsNull);
  criteria:=filter(aWeek, criteria);
  projRes:=criteria.UniqueValue;

  ...    lbAnswerSpeedValue.Text:=FormatDateTime('n:ss',projres.
         Values['AnswerSpeed']);
  ...

  projRes.Free;
end;
```

We have seen this pattern before; we use the Avg function of Aurelius and the IsNull condition to filter the entities. This time we pass a calculation (the subtraction) directly in a function and, finally, present the result in the right format. This snippet also shows that Aurelius is capable of managing different data types in a simple way.

Abandon Rate

This rate shows the percentage of the calls that reach the center but are not completed for any reason. For such calls, the system records an entry time, but the exit time from the queue is null. Therefore, we need to get the number of calls for which the `QueueExitTime` is null and divide it by the total calls the center received. We have stored this value in `totalCalls`. Thus, we would like Aurelius to calculate in a projection the following division:

```
TProjections.Count('ID') / totalCalls
```

and place it in an Add call:

```
.Add(TProjections.Count('ID') / totalCalls)
```

If you try this, the compiler will throw an error complaining that `totalCalls` is not of `TSimpleProjection` type as expected but an `integer` (constant). This is correct as Aurelius, internally, manages operations in projections that derive from `TSimpleProjection`. `Literal<T>` function comes to rescue as it can convert a constant to the correct type and can be used safely as part of the projections list. In our case, we convert `totalCalls` to a compatible form using the following code:

```
TProjections.Literal<integer>(totalCalls)
```

The final code to calculate and display the abandon rate takes the following form:

```
procedure TFormMain.calculateStatistics(const aWeek: TWeeks);
var
  ...
begin
  ...
  criteria:=session.objectManager.Find<TCall>
                         .Select(TProjections.
                         ProjectionList
```

```
                              .Add(TProjections.Divide(
  TProjections.Count('ID') , TProjections.Literal<Integer>
  (totalCalls))

                                      .As_('AbandonRate'))
                            )
                            .Where(Linq['QueueExitTime'].
                            IsNull);
  criteria:=filter(aWeek, criteria);
  projRes:=criteria.UniqueValue;

...  lbAbandonRateValue.Text:=format('%3.2f',[Double(projres.
     Values['AbandonRate']) * 100]);
  ...

  projRes.Free;
end;
```

Calls/Minute

This is the number of calls the center receives divided by the total operation time of the center. Data reveals that the center is open between 09:00 and 18:00 (9 hours). Therefore, the calculation of this metrics is simple.

```
procedure TFormMain.calculateStatistics(const aWeek: TWeeks);
var
  ...
begin
  ...
  lbCallsMinuteValue.Text:=format('%3.2f',[ totalCalls / 9 / 60]);
end;
```

Calls Answered in Less Than 180 Seconds

This indicator shows the calls that stayed in the queue for less than 3 minutes. In terms of calculations, we need to work out the difference between the times the calls entered and exited the queue and, then, pick those where the difference is less than 180 seconds. By now, we have all the building blocks to write this Aurelius projection.

```
procedure TFormMain.calculateStatistics(const aWeek: TWeeks);
var
  ...
begin
  ...
  criteria:=session.objectManager.Find<TCall>
                            .Select(TProjections.
                            ProjectionList
                     .Add(TProjections.Count('ID').
                     As_('CallsLess180'))
                            )
                            .Where(
           (Linq['QueueExitTime'] - Linq['QueueEntryTime']) <
                                       EncodeTime(0, 3, 0, 0))
                            .Where(not Linq
                            ['QueueExitTime'].IsNull);
  criteria:=filter(aWeek, criteria);
  projRes:=criteria.UniqueValue;

  ...
  lbAnsweredLess180.Text:=projres.Values['CallsLess180'];

  ...

  projRes.Free;
end;
```

The only, perhaps, new element we have is that we can use computational conditions in a Where statement as the code shows. I encoded the 180 seconds limit as a time object.

Calls with Satisfactory Score Less Than 3

This time we are looking at the calls with satisfactory score less than 3. We need the absolute number and the fraction of these calls that correspond to the total calls. We are able to extract both pieces of data, directly, from the database using familiar methods. In this case, though, note how we can add more than one projection function in the same query. This is because we constantly use TProjections.ProjectionList to create the queries.

```
procedure TFormMain.calculateStatistics(const aWeek: TWeeks);
var
  ...
begin
  ...
  criteria:=session.objectManager.Find<TCall>
                            .Select(TProjections.
                            ProjectionList
              .Add(TProjections.Count('ID').
              As_('CallsLess3'))
              .Add(TProjections.Divide(
                      TProjections.Count('ID'),
                      TProjections.
                      Literal<Integer>(totalCalls)
                 .As_('CallsLess3Perc'))
                 )
```

```
                    .Where(not Linq['QueueExitTime'].IsNull)
                    .Where(Linq['SatisfactionScore'] < 3);
  criteria:=filter(aWeek, criteria);
  projRes:=criteria.UniqueValue;

  ...
  lbSatisfactionScoreLess3.Text:= format('%d (%3.2f%%)',
              [integer(projres.Values['CallsLess3']),
                double(projres.Values['CallsLess3Perc']) * 100]);

  ...

  projRes.Free;
end;
```

Agent Statistics List

The list with the statistics per agent can be completed by making similar calls to Aurelius. The requirement this time is that we need aggregated results per individual agent, or, in other words, we need to group the results per agent. This can be achieved by adding a call to Group function inside the projection.

```
procedure TFormMain.calculateStatistics(const aWeek: TWeeks);
var
  ...
begin
  ...
  criteria:=session.objectManager.Find<TCall>
                            .CreateAlias('AgentID',
                            'agent')
                            .Select(TProjections.
                            ProjectionList
```

```
                    .Add(TProjections.
                    Prop('agent.Description').
                    As_('Name'))
                    .Add(TProjections.
                    Count('ID').As_
                    ('TotalCalls'))
                    .Add(TProjections.
                    Group('agent.ID'))
                )
                .OrderBy('agent.Description');
    criteria:=filter(aWeek, criteria);
    agentList:=criteria.ListValues;
end;
```

The code groups the calls to Count by the ID of the agents. Note the way we access the ID property; the AgentID property in TCall is an entity itself, and therefore if we want to drill down to its properties, we need to create an alias pointing to TAgent. Then, we can use this alias inside projection calls in the same way we used it when we were dealing with criteria. We, also, want to show the name of the agent as appears in the Description field. As this is a simple use of a field from the main table, it can be easily access using the Prop function.

This snippet calculates the total calls for each agent. The other indicators in the agent list are determined in a similar manner. I do not show the code here, as it would be a repetition of what we have already seen. If you wish to see the full implementation, please refer to the code files that accompany this book.

Views

We implemented the dashboard screen by running several database queries in order to extract all the necessary data. In some instances, we had to do calculations in code before being able to present the right data. This is a very common approach but, in some instances, may not be ideal. For example, if the data set is huge or the resources are limited as it happens in mobile platforms, or if there are security concerns and, perhaps, legacy database schema, it is, strongly, preferable to allow the database engine to handle the queries.

In Aurelius, we can use Views very easily. In fact, Aurelius manages views in the same way as entities. This is very advantageous; we already know how to manage entities. The only difference at this stage is that views are *read-only* as the whole definition of views suggests. For the CallCentre project, we are going to define the TOverallStatistics entity to represent the OverallStatistics view. The code of this section is under *Call Centre – Views* folder.

1. Open Entities.pas unit and add the following class:

```
...
interface
...
type
  ...
  [Entity]
  [Table('OverallStatistics')]
  [Id('FWeek', TIdGenerator.None)]
  TOverallStatistics = class
  private
    [Column('Week', [TColumnProp.Required])]
    FWeek: Integer;
```

```
  [Column('SatisfactionScore', [TColumnProp.Required])]
  FSatisfactionScore: Double;

  [Column('TotalCalls', [TColumnProp.Required])]
  FTotalCalls: Integer;

  [Column('AnswerSpeed', [TColumnProp.Required])]
  FAnswerSpeed: Double;

  [Column('AbandonRate', [TColumnProp.Required])]
  FAbandonRate: Double;

  [Column('CallsMinute', [TColumnProp.Required])]
  FCallsMinute: Double;

  [Column('CallsLess180', [TColumnProp.Required])]
  FCallsLess180: Integer;

  [Column('CallsLess3', [TColumnProp.Required])]
  FCallsLess3: Integer;

  [Column('CallsLess3Perc', [TColumnProp.Required])]
  FCallsLess3Perc: Double;
public
  property Week: Integer read FWeek write FWeek;
  property SatisfactionScore: Double read FSatisfactionScore
  write FSatisfactionScore;
  property TotalCalls: Integer read FTotalCalls write
  FTotalCalls;
  property AnswerSpeed: Double read FAnswerSpeed write
  FAnswerSpeed;
  property AbandonRate: Double read FAbandonRate write
  FAbandonRate;
  property CallsMinute: Double read FCallsMinute write
  FCallsMinute;
```

```
property CallsLess180: Integer read FCallsLess180 write
FCallsLess180;
property CallsLess3: Integer read FCallsLess3 write
FCallsLess3;
property CallsLess3Perc: Double read FCallsLess3Perc write
FCallsLess3Perc;
end;
```

...

There are a few points to mention about this entity that represents a view. First, the primary key (Week) is linked to one of the columns of the view. This is only to provide a unique identifier to the entity to keep Aurelius happy. The second point follows the first one. All the properties in this entity are flagged as required but again this is not important. I chose to do this because I do not want to check whether a property has content as we do when we deal with nullable fields. Unless the view is empty, I can, simply, use the property values. The last point to mention has to do with the naming and data type of the properties. This entity represents a view in the database and, therefore, the properties and the data types must be the same (or compatible) to the columns in the actual view.

2. Run the CallCentre application. Aurelius will go on and create a table named OverallStatistics when updateDatabase is called. But this is not what we want to achieve. Aurelius may treat OverallStatistics as an entity (table) but, at database level, it is a view. This homogenous

approach, also, leaves us unable to rely to Aurelius schema management to create or update a view. We rather need to do this manually.

3. Delete the table, drop the database, or delete the database file. Let's start clean.

4. In order to prevent Aurelius checking for OverallStatistics table and from creating it, we need the help of models. The idea of models in Aurelius allows developers to create conceptual group entities (tables) to serve different tasks. A very common use of models is to separate the tables that hold security, licensing, or user management data from the main (default) group of tables. Models can go beyond conceptual level and be associated to different databases. Therefore, for instance, you can have two databases: one for the licensing and another for the application-specific data.

   In our application, we are going to introduce the Database model to organize those entities that reflect views. Go back to TOverallStatistics class and decorate it with the attribute Model.

```
type
  ...
  [Entity]
  [Table('OverallStatistics')]
  [Model('Database')]
  [Id('FWeek', TIdGenerator.None)]
  TOverallStatistics = class
    ...
  end;
```

5. Run the application again. If you look at the
    database, you will see that Aurelius did not create
    the TOverallStatistics table because, the way we
    have set things up, the main (default) model is used.
    If you do not provide the Model attribute to an entity,
    it is considered part of the Default model.

6. We now need to create the view in the database.
    If you have the option and access, you can run the
    following SQL script manually to do this. The script
    can be found in the Misc folder in the code files under
    the name OverallStatisticsViewScript.sql.

```sql
CREATE VIEW IF NOT EXISTS OverallStatistics AS select
        Week,
        Avg(SatisfactionScore) as SatisfactionScore,
        Count(*) as TotalCalls,
        (Avg( case
                when QueueExitTime is not null then
                QueueExitTime - QueueEntryTime
              end )) as AnswerSpeed,
        (Count( case
                when QueueExitTime is null then 1
              end ) * 100.0 ) / count(*) as AbandonRate,
        (Count(*) / 9.00 / 60.00) as CallsMinute,
        (Count ( case
                when (QueueExitTime is not null) and
                ((QueueExitTime - QueueEntryTime) <
                0.00208333333333333) then 1
              end )) as CallsLess180,
        (Count( case
                when SatisfactionScore < 3 then 1
              end )) as CallsLess3,
```

```
    (Count( case
                when SatisfactionScore < 3 then 1
            end ) * 100.0 / count(*) ) as CallsLess3Perc
from
  Call

GROUP BY
  Week;
```

7. In the case you cannot manage the database directly or in situations where you want your applications to update the database, you need to execute the script using Aurelius features.

8. Aurelius defines the IDBStatement interface, which allows us to pass plain SQL statements and execute them directly. This takes place at the TObjectManager level. Add the next private method in TFormMain in MainForm.pas. Note that you need to add Database.Session.Types in the interface section now.

```
uses
  ...,
  Database.Session.Types;
type
  TFormMain = class(TForm)
  ...
  private
  ...
    procedure createViews(const dbSession: IDatabaseSession);
  end;
```

...

implementation

...

```
procedure TFormMain.createViews(const dbSession:
IDatabaseSession);
var
  statement: IDBStatement;
  sqlScript: string;
begin
  sqlScript:=
  'CREATE VIEW IF NOT EXISTS OverallStatistics AS select' +
  '  Week,' +
  '  avg(SatisfactionScore) as SatisfactionScore,' +
  '  Count(*) as TotalCalls,' +
  '  (Avg( case' +
  '           when QueueExitTime is not null then
             QueueExitTime - QueueEntryTime' +
  '         end )) as AnswerSpeed,' +
  '  (Count( case' +
  '            when QueueExitTime is null then 1' +
  '          end ) * 100.0 ) / count(*) as AbandonRate,' +
  '  (Count(*) / 9.00 / 60.00) as CallsMinute,' +
  '  (Count ( case' +
  '             when (QueueExitTime is not null) and
               ((QueueExitTime - QueueEntryTime) <
               0.002083333333333333) then 1' +
  '           end )) as CallsLess180,' +
  '  (Count( case' +
  '            when SatisfactionScore < 3 then 1' +
  '          end )) as CallsLess3,' +
```

```
'   (Count( case' +
'              when SatisfactionScore < 3 then 1' +
'            end ) * 100.0 / count(*) ) as CallsLess3Perc ' +
'FROM' +
'   Call ' +
'GROUP BY' +
'   Week;';

statement:=dbSession.objectManager.Connection.CreateStatement;
statement.SetSQLCommand(sqlScript);
statement.Execute;
end;
```

We declare an IDBStatement variable, and we use the CreateStatement function to instantiate it. Then, we load the script to the interface using SetSQLCommand and finally execute it. In a full-scale application, most likely you want to wrap statement.Execute in a try-except branch.

In the preceding snippet, I have added some spaces to make the SQL script readable. Obviously, this is not necessary, as it is just a script. What matters, though, is the space at the beginning (or the end) of each line if you choose to create this concatenated string as I have done. Otherwise, you will end up with a script with adjacent words without any spaces.

9.   Go to FormCreate event in MainForm.pas and call createViews:

```
uses
  ...
  Aurelius.Drivers.Interfaces;
...
procedure TFormMain.FormCreate(Sender: TObject);
...
begin
  ...
  dbSession.databaseManager.UpdateDatabase;

  createViews(dbSession);

  setupGUI;
end;
```

10. If you check the code in the supplied files, I have added the same code in the procedure that executes the importing of the data. I will not mention it here as it is the same as the preceding snippet.

11. Time to get our data from the view and show it in the dashboard. Go to calculateStatistics in TFormMain and retrieve the list of entities:

```
procedure TFormMain.calculateStatistics(const aWeek: TWeeks);
var
  session: IDatabaseSession;
  overallStatsList: TList<TOverallStatistics>;
begin
  session:=TDatabaseSession.Create(SQLiteConnection.CreateConnection);

  overallStatsList:=session.objectManager.
  Find<TOverallStatistics>.List;

    overallStatsList.Free;
end;
```

12. As you can see, accessing a view in Aurelius is done in the same way as accessing every other entity. However, the preceding code breaks. Try to execute it and you will see that Aurelius complains with the message of *"Class TOverallStatistics is not a valid Entity. [Entity] attribute missing."* although we have used `Entity` attribute in the class.

13. The reason for this error message is that we have made `TOverallStatistics` part of `Database` model. The call to `Find` in the preceding code accesses the `Default` model. We need to instruct the object manager to look at the `Database` model.

14. Open `Database.Session.Types.pas` and add the following overloading function to `IDatabaseSession`:

```
type
  IDatabaseSession = interface
    ...
    function objectManager: TObjectManager; overload;
    function objectManager (const aModel: string):
    TObjectManager; overload;
  end;
```

15. In `Database.Session.pas`, add the implementation of the function. In this example, I have introduced a dictionary to hold the different object managers based on the model they serve. This can be handy when multiple models are present. The following code shows the full unit and highlights the differences from before:

```
unit Database.Session;

interface

uses
  Database.Session.Types,
  Aurelius.Engine.DatabaseManager,
  Aurelius.Drivers.Interfaces,
  Aurelius.Engine.ObjectManager, System.Generics.Collections;

type
  TDatabaseSession = class (TInterfacedObject,
  IDatabaseSession)
  private
    fConnection: IDBConnection;
    fDatabaseManager: TDatabaseManager;
    fObjectManagerDictionary: TObjectDictionary<string,
    TObjectManager>;
  public
    constructor Create(const aConnection: IDBConnection);
    destructor Destroy; override;
{$REGION 'Interface'}
    function databaseManager: TDatabaseManager;
    function objectManager: TObjectManager; overload;
    function objectManager (const aModel: string): TObjectManager;
    overload;
{$ENDREGION}
  end;

implementation

uses
  System.SysUtils, Aurelius.Mapping.Explorer;
```

```
constructor TDatabaseSession.Create(const aConnection:
IDBConnection);
begin
  Assert(aConnection <> nil);

  inherited Create;
  fConnection:=aConnection;
  fObjectManagerDictionary:=TObjectDictionary<string,
  TObjectManager>.Create([doOwnsValues]);
end;

function TDatabaseSession.databaseManager: TDatabaseManager;
begin
  if not Assigned(fDatabaseManager) then
    fDatabaseManager:=TDatabaseManager.Create(fConnection);
  Result:=fDatabaseManager;
end;

destructor TDatabaseSession.Destroy;
begin
  fDatabaseManager.Free;
  fObjectManagerDictionary.Free;
  inherited;
end;

function TDatabaseSession.objectManager(const aModel: string):
TObjectManager;
var
  cModel: string;
begin
  cModel:=Trim(UpperCase(aModel));
  if cModel=" then
    Result:=objectManager
```

```
  else
  begin
    if not fObjectManagerDictionary.ContainsKey(cModel) then
      if cModel = 'DEFAULT' then
        fObjectManagerDictionary.Add('DEFAULT', TObjectManager.
        Create(fConnection))
      else
        fObjectManagerDictionary.Add(cModel,
              TObjectManager.Create(fConnection,
              TMappingExplorer.Get(cModel)));
    Result:=fObjectManagerDictionary.Items[cModel];
  end;
end;

function TDatabaseSession.objectManager: TObjectManager;
begin
  result:=objectManager('default');
end;

end.
```

We create a new instance of object manager for each model. A simple call to the constructor of TObjectManager passes the Default model. When we need an object manager for specific model other than the default, we use TMappingExplorer to provide the internal structure of the database representation we are interested in. TMappingExplorer is responsible for scanning through entities attached to a database model.

16. Now we are ready to access the content of the view. We also factor in the filtering according to the week.

```
procedure TFormMain.calculateStatistics(const aWeek: TWeeks);
var
  ...,
  criteria: TCriteria;
  overallStatsList: TList<TOverallStatistics>;
begin
  session:=TDatabaseSession.Create(SQLiteConnection.
  CreateConnection);

  criteria:=session.objectManager('Database').
  Find<TOverallStatistics>;
  criteria:=filter(aWeek, criteria);
  overallStatsList:=criteria.List<TOverallStatistics>;

    overallStatsList.Free;
end;
```

> We pass the name of the model (Database) to the
> object manager, and we use filter to generate the
> correct call according to the chosen week. Then,
> we retrieve the content of the view and assign it to
> overallStatsList. Note that we need to provide the
> exact data type to List<> because we, now, do not
> retrieve a list of criteria results, as we did previously.

17. From this point onward, we can easily access the
    results and update the dashboard.

```
procedure TFormMain.calculateStatistics(const aWeek: TWeeks);
var
  ...,
  overallStats: TOverallStatistics;
begin
```

```
session:=TDatabaseSession.Create(SQLiteConnection.
CreateConnection);

criteria:=session.objectManager('Database').
Find<TOverallStatistics>;
criteria:=filter(aWeek, criteria);
overallStatsList:=criteria.List<TOverallStatistics>;
...

for overallStats in overallStatsList do
begin
  lbSatisfactionValue.Text:=format('%2.2f', [overallStats.
  SatisfactionScore]);
  lbTotalCallsValue.Text:= overallStats.TotalCalls.ToString;
  lbAnswerSpeedValue.Text:=FormatDateTime('n:ss',
  overallStats.AnswerSpeed);
  lbAbandonRateValue.Text:=format('%3.2f%%', [overallStats.
  AbandonRate]);
  lbCallsMinuteValue.Text:=format('%3.2f', [overallStats.
  CallsMinute]);
  lbAnsweredLess180Value.Text:= overallStats.CallsLess180.
  ToString;
    lbSatisfactionScoreLess3Value.Text:= format('%d (%3.2f%%)',
             [overallStats.CallsLess3,
               overallStats.CallsLess3Perc * 100]);
  end;
  ...

  overallStatsList.Free;
end;
```

Note   The preceding code is different from the one you can find in the code files. In the actual code, we need to manage the fact that we present the results of week 4 and week 5 consolidated.

Summary

In this chapter, we covered lot of ground. We started with simple queries to get lists of agents and departments, and we moved on to explore how we can build complex requests and take advantage of Aurelius' fluent interface. We also saw how the framework provides options for calculations and grouping. The last topic we discussed was database views – a way to move heavy calculations totally to the server side and, consequently, take advantage of the database engine.

CHAPTER 6

Enhancements

Our application has now most of its core functionality. It manages agents and departments and shows the majority of the key performance indicators and statistics. There are a few more bits to complete. In this chapter, we will finish them and demonstrate some additional features of Aurelius.

Inheritance

Inheritance is one of the most widely used features of OOP. It is useful in numerous cases; it saves time and effort and, above all, leads to well-designed object systems that support complicated concepts. Inheritance, at the same time, poses a problem for database administrators. The way inherited objects can be stored and retrieved in a database is the topic of an almost ongoing debate. This case is an example where the way developers think does not, easily, map to database structure.

Aurelius allows developers to design their classes in any way they need and prefer, and then the framework takes responsibility and, with minimum modifications, entities can be easily managed. In order to understand how this works, we will add to our database information about who (user) and when (date/timestamp) an entry was created and modified. This is a common set of fields that can (or should) be present in all the tables, but to keep things simple and clean we will implement it for the TAgent table only. You may have already noticed that, in the MainForm, we have already added the fields to display this information. As before, please check the *Call Centre – Inheritance* for the code.

© John Kouraklis 2019
J. Kouraklis, *Introducing Delphi ORM*, https://doi.org/10.1007/978-1-4842-5013-6_6

Consistent to OOP design, we would create a TBase class with the following blueprint:

```
type
  TBase = class
  private
    FCreateUser: string;
    FCreateTS: TDateTime;
    FModifyUser: string;
    FModifyTS: TDateTime;
  public
    property CreateUser: string read FCreateUser write FCreateUser;
    property CreateTS: TDateTime read FCreateTS write FCreateTS;
    property ModifyUser: string read FModifyUser write FModifyUser;
    property ModifyTS: TDateTime read FModifyTS write FModifyTS;
  end;
```

Then, we would inherit TAgent from TBase to make the preceding properties available to TAgent.

```
TAgent = class (TBase)
...
end;
```

The next step is to inform Aurelius there is an entity that inherits properties from another one. This is, naturally, done with the use of appropriate attributes that decorate the classes. There are two options when it comes to inheritance in Aurelius: to represent it as a single table in the database or to normalize the database and create linked tables. There are both pros and cons for these two approaches; please refer to the manual for details.

Single table (SingleTable) inheritance means that Aurelius picks all the inherited entities which have the same ancestor class and stores all the values from all the classes (both the ancestor and the inherited) in one single table in the database. You manage the entities in your code as you normally do. You cannot see any difference. It is, only, when they inspect the database itself that you observe the structure (Figure 6-1).

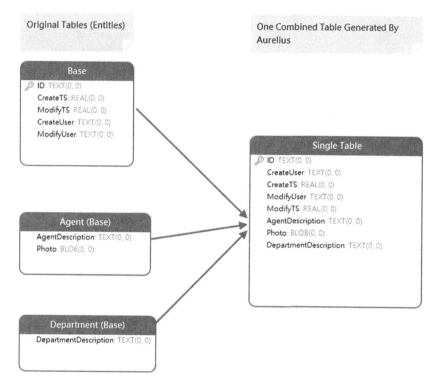

Figure 6-1. *Single table inheritance database model*

In the figure, the TAgent and TDepartment entities inherit from TBase class. Aurelius puts all the fields in one table and adds a discriminatory column, which allows it to retrieve the correct values. Note that since all the fields are consolidated in one table, you cannot have fields with the same name (compare AgentDescription and DepartmentDescription to Description fields in the original classes). Additionally, the primary fields (ID) are removed from the successors, and it is only required in the TBase class.

For CallCentre application, we are going to implement the second method that uses linked or joint tables (JoinedTables). We start from the inherited entity and the base class, and Aurelius creates an equivalent table structure in the database (Figure 6-2).

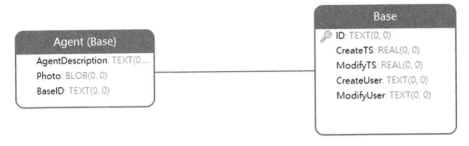

Figure 6-2. *Joint table inheritance database model*

1. In Entities.pas, go to TBase class and decorate it with the Inheritance attribute to indicate that we want the JointTable strategy to be implemented. In the following code snippet, I have also added all the attributes to configure the entity for use by Aurelius:

```
...
type
  [Entity]
  [Table('Base')]
  [Id('FID', TIdGenerator.Guid)]
  [Inheritance(TInheritanceStrategy.JoinedTables)]
  TBase = class
  private
    [Column('ID', [TColumnProp.Required])]
    FID: TGuid;
```

```
    [Column('CreateUser', [], 50)]
    FCreateUser: Nullable<string>;

    [Column('CreateTS', [])]
    FCreateTS: Nullable<TDateTime>;

    [Column('ModifyUser', [], 50)]
    FModifyUser: Nullable<string>;

    [Column('ModifyTS', [])]
    FModifyTS: Nullable<TDateTime>;
  public
    property ID: TGuid read FID write FID;
    property CreateUser: Nullable<string> read FCreateUser
    write FCreateUser;
    property CreateTS: Nullable<TDateTime> read FCreateTS write
    FCreateTS;
    property ModifyUser: Nullable<string> read FModifyUser
    write FModifyUser;
    property ModifyTS: Nullable<TDateTime> read FModifyTS write
    FModifyTS;
  end;
...
initialization
  ...
  RegisterEntity(TBase);
...
end.
```

> 2. TBase is the ancestor class; now, we need to move to the inherited class (TAgent) and add the PrimaryJoinColumn attribute.

```
...
type
  ...
  [Entity]
  [Table('Agent')]
  [PrimaryJoinColumn('BaseID')]
// [Id('FID', TIdGenerator.Guid)]              Delete these lines
  TAgent = class (TBase)
  private
//    [Column('ID', [TColumnProp.Required])]
//    FID: TGuid;
    ...
  public
    ...
//    property ID: TGuid read FID write FID;
    ...
  end;
```

> We, also, need to delete the primary key property (lines in comment tags) because TAgent inherits the ID property from TBase class; Aurelius uses the primary key of the ancestor as the primary key of the successor. The two entities are now linked in the code level, but they are separate tables at database level. The question arises about how Aurelius is able to link the two. The answer is provided by the PrimaryJoinColumn attribute; in the example, we pass BaseID and we, effectively, indicate to the framework that a new field named BaseID will be the foreign key for the Base table. If PrimaryJoinColumn is omitted, Aurelius assumes the name of the identifier field.

3. Removing the primary key from TAgent has the
    knock-off effect of destroying any associations
    in which TAgent is involved unless we omit
    PrimaryJoinColumn. We need to update them and
    use BaseID instead.

4. In MainForm.pas, populate the CreateUser and
    ModifyUser to reflect the name of the user and
    the actions. As a simple approach, we use the user
    "user" when the user adds or modifies an agent and
    the user *"system"* when we import entities from
    external sources.

```
procedure TFormMain.btAddAgentClick(Sender: TObject);
...
begin

  ...
  if form.ShowModal = mrOk then
  begin

session:=TDatabaseSession.Create(SQLiteConnection.
CreateConnection);
    agent:=TAgent.Create;
    agent.Description:=Trim(form.edEntity.Text);
    agent.CreateUser:='user';

    TDatabaseUtilities<TAgent>.edit(session.objectManager, agent);

    updateAgents;

  end;
  ...
end;

...
```

```
procedure TFormMain.btEditAgentClick(Sender: TObject);
...
begin
  ...
  if Assigned(agent) then
  begin
    ...
    if form.ShowModal = mrOk then
    begin
      agent.Description:=Trim(form.edEntity.Text);
      agent.ModifyUser:='user';

      TDatabaseUtilities<TAgent>.edit(session.objectManager, agent);

      updateAgents;
    end;
    ...
  end;
end;
```

5. In Database.Import.pas, update CreateUser field
   to system.

```
procedure importData (const aFilename: string; const
aConnection: IDBConnection; const aImportFrame: TFrameImport);
...
begin
  ...
  for agentName in agentsDictionary.Keys do
  begin
    agent:=TAgent.Create;
    agent.Description:=agentName;
    ...
```

```
    TDatabaseUtilities<TAgent>.bitmapToBlob(agentPhoto, 'png',
    agentBlob);
    agent.Photo:=agentBlob;
    agent.CreateUser:='system';
    ...
  end;
  ...
end;
```

6. Back in MainForm.pas, create a new procedure to show these fields to the form.

```
interface
...
type
  TFormMain = class(TForm)
    ...
  private
    ...
    procedure loadAgentMetadata (const aGUID: string);
  public
    ...
  end;
...
implementation
...
procedure TFormMain.loadAgentMetadata(const aGUID: string);
var
  session: IDatabaseSession;
  agent: TAgent;
begin
  Assert(Trim(aGUID) <> ");
```

```
session:=TDatabaseSession.Create(SQLiteConnection.
CreateConnection);
agent:=session.objectManager.Find<TAgent>(Trim(aGUID));

  if Assigned(agent) then
  begin
  if agent.CreateUser.HasValue then
    lbCreateUser.Text:=agent.CreateUser.Value
  else
    lbCreateUser.Text:='Not Assigned';

  if agent.ModifyUser.HasValue then
    lbModifyUser.Text:=agent.ModifyUser.Value
  else
    lbModifyUser.Text:='Not Assigned';

  if agent.CreateTS.HasValue then
    lbCreateTS.Text:=FormatDateTime('DD/MM/YYYY, HH:MM',
    agent.CreateTS.Value)
  else
    lbCreateTS.Text:='Not Assigned';

  if agent.ModifyTS.HasValue then
    lbModifyTS.Text:=FormatDateTime('DD/MM/YYYY, HH:MM ',
    agent.ModifyTS.Value)
  else
    lbModifyTS.Text:='Not Assigned';
  end;
end;
```

7. In OnSelectCell event of the agent's grid, call loadAgentMetadata to update the form.

```
procedure TFormMain.sgAgentsSelectCell (Sender: TObject; const ACol, ARow:
    Integer; var CanSelect: Boolean);
begin
  ...
  loadAgentMetadata(sgAgents.Cells[2, ARow]);

  updateAgentList;
end;
```

Events

When we used inheritance to keep track of the user who creates and updates an agent, we did not touch the timestamps of those actions. Obviously, it is very simple to add two or three lines to populate the *create* and *modify* timestamp fields. In this case, however, we are going to turn our attention to Aurelius events. Events is a general term used in software engineering that indicates a mechanism where several entities exchange messages.

Aurelius comes with such a system. The framework posts events as a result of basic actions (insert, update, delete) that take place in a database. For an up-to-date list of the available events, please refer to the technical manual. The general course of actions in relation to the events follows these steps:

1. The application that uses Aurelius provides a callback procedure and attaches (subscribes) it to the events manager.

2. Every time the application performs a transaction in the database, Aurelius event manager posts a message to the subscribers by triggering the callback procedure.

177

3. The callback procedure gives to the application access to the entities and other details related to the transaction.

4. When it is suitable (e.g., when the application exits), the application should unsubscribe from Aurelius events mechanism.

OnInserting and OnUpdating Events

As you may have guessed, we are going to use events to update the timestamps in our database and, in particular, the OnInserting and OnUpdating, which occur right before an entity is saved or updated. "*Right before*" in this instance means that Aurelius has completed any processing of the entity and it is ready to hit the database. The code of this part is available in the *Call Centre – Events* folder.

1. Add a new unit to the project and save it as Database.Events.Types.pas and declare the IDatabaseEvents interface.

```
unit Database.Events.Types;

interface

type
  IDatabaseEvents = interface
    ['{369927E5-976A-4263-9E66-31355C3E7C2C}']
    procedure subscribeEvents;
    procedure unsubscribeEvents;
  end;

implementation

end.
```

2.   Add another unit under the name Database.
     Events.pas and add the following code:

```
unit Database.Events;

interface

uses
  Database.Events.Types,
  Aurelius.Events.Manager;

type
  TDatabaseEvents = class (TInterfacedObject, IDatabaseEvents)
  private
    fInsertingProc: TInsertingProc;
    fUpdatingProc: TUpdatingProc;
  public
    procedure subscribeEvents;
    procedure unsubscribeEvents;
  end;

implementation

end.
```

In the implementation of IDatabaseEvents
interface, we declare the two procedures that allow
us to subscribe and unsubscribe to Aurelius' event
manager. We also declare two private variables
(fInsertingProc and fUpdatingProc) that
represent the callback procedure; that is, when
an entity is about to be inserted or updated in the
database, Aurelius will trigger these two procedures.

3. Registering (and unregistering) them is done in the
    following code:

```
unit Database.Events;

interface

...

implementation

uses
  Aurelius.Mapping.Explorer;

procedure TDatabaseEvents.subscribeEvents;
begin
  TMappingExplorer.Default.Events.OnInserting.Subscribe
  (fInsertingProc);

  TMappingExplorer.Default.Events.OnUpdating.Subscribe
  (fUpdatingProc);
end;

procedure TDatabaseEvents.unsubscribeEvents;
begin
  TMappingExplorer.Default.Events.OnInserting.Unsubscribe
  (fInsertingProc);

  TMappingExplorer.Default.Events.OnUpdating.Unsubscribe
  (fUpdatingProc);
end;

end.
```

We have come across the mapping explorer before
when we dealt with the views and different database
scheme models. We use the OnInserting and
OnUpdating gateways from the Events property of the

`TMappingExplorer` to subscribe (and unsubscribe) our custom callback procedures to Aurelius.

If you check the technical manual, you may notice that you can pass an anonymous method directly to the `Subscribe` and `Unsubscribe` methods of the mapping explorer, which eliminates the need for separate variables. The reason I chose to introduce the variables is that I want to be able to clean up the procedures manually rather than rely to the framework to nil-ify them. This is more of a personal choice that I feel leads to good coding practice but, admittedly, without any strong advantages to support this argument.

One last note worth mentioning: as you can see in the code, we attached the callback procedures to the `Default` model of the database. This means that our procedures will be triggered only when an entity in our default model is involved in a transaction. In our case, thankfully, we only have the view definition outside the default model, so we are safe.

You may, however, have a different situation in a full-scale application. It was mentioned before that models can be useful to organize database scheme, and a common use is to group together entities related to security and authorization. Attaching the events to the default model will isolate any triggering from the `Security` model entities, as an example. If you want to subscribe and unsubscribe events in a different model, you can do it as in the following code:

```
TMappingExplorer.Get('Security').Events.OnInserting.
Subscribe(fInsertingProc);
```

4. It is time now to define our event procedures.
    Add a typical constructor and destructor to the
    TDatabaseEvent class and define fInsertingProc.

```
unit Database.Events;

interface

...

type
  TDatabaseEvents = class (TInterfacedObject, IDatabaseEvents)
  private

    ...

  public
    constructor Create;

    ...

  end;

implementation

uses
  ...,
  Entities,
  System.SysUtils,
  Aurelius.Mapping.Explorer;

constructor TDatabaseEvents.Create;
begin
  inherited;
  fInsertingProc:= procedure (Args: TInsertingArgs)
                begin
                  if Args.Entity is TAgent then
                  begin
                    (Args.Entity as TAgent).CreateTS:=Now;
                  end;
                end;
end;
```

We use the TInsertingArgs in the declaration of our procedure. TInsertingArgs provides details about the entity and the object manager that are involved in the database transaction that triggers this event.

As we are interested in updating the agents' data, we filter the calls by checking that the TInsertingArgs. Entity property is of TAgent. When the correct entity is identified, we update the CreateTS field.

5. In a similar way, we define the fUpdatingProc and populate the ModifyTS field.

```
unit Database.Events;

interface
...
implementation
...
constructor TDatabaseEvents.Create;
...
begin
  ...
  fUpdatingProc:= procedure (Args: TUpdatingArgs)
              begin
                if Args.Entity is TAgent then
                begin
                  (Args.Entity as TAgent).ModifyTS:=Now;
                  Args.RecalculateState:=True;
                end;
              end;
end;
```

6. This procedure is the same as before with only one subtle but important difference. When Aurelius triggers an `OnUpdating` event, it has completed the mapping of the entity and the parsing of any changes, and it is ready to push the modifications to the database. If you inspect `Args.OldColumnValues` and `Args.NewColumnValues` properties, you can identify the changes in the entity. However, this opens up a gap; if any changes of entity's properties take place in the event itself, as we do in the preceding code, Aurelius misses the opportunity to consume the modifications, and consequently these changes will not be saved in the database. The way to resolve this is to set `Args.RecalculateState` to true as this property will force Aurelius to reparse the entity.

7. In the destructor, we clean things up by unsubscribing the procedures from the events manager and setting them to `nil`.

```
...
type
  TDatabaseEvents = class (TInterfacedObject, IDatabaseEvents)
  private
    ...
  public
    destructor Destroy; override;
    ...
  end;

implementation
...
```

```
destructor TDatabaseEvents.Destroy;
begin
  unsubscribeEvents;
  fInsertingProc:=nil;
  fUpdatingProc:=nil;
  inherited;
end;
```

8. The last thing left to do is to manage thc events in the main form. Open MainForm.pas and update the OnCreate event. Similarly, amend the code in the OnDestroy event of the form as follows:

```
unit MainForm;

interface

uses
  ...,
  Database.Events.Types;

type
  ...
  TFormMain = class(TForm)
    ...
  private
    dbEvents: IDatabaseEvents;
    ...
  end;
...
implementation

uses
  ...,
  Database.Events;
```

```
procedure TFormMain.FormCreate(Sender: TObject);

...

begin

  ...

  dbEvents:=TDatabaseEvents.Create;
  dbEvents.subscribeEvents;

  setupGUI;
end;

procedure TFormMain.FormDestroy(Sender: TObject);
begin

  ...

  dbEvents.unsubscribeEvents;
end;
```

OnInserted and OnUpdated Events

Aurelius triggers OnInserted and OnUpdated events after the operations
in the underlying database have been completed, offering a window to
postprocess the entities. In this small section, we will see how we can
update CreateTS and ModifyTS using these events. The code is more
convoluted compared to the simple approach in the previous section.
Nevertheless, this part shows how you can use these events to modify
entities that have just been stored in the database. You can find this code in
Database.Events.Alternative.pas file in the code.

1. We first declare two variables to hold the event
   procedures.

```
unit Database.Events.Alternative;

interface

...
```

```
type
  TDatabaseEvents = class (TInterfacedObject, IDatabaseEvents)
  private
    fInsertedProc: TInsertedProc;
    fUpdatedProc: TUpdatedProc;
  public
    ...
  end;
```

2.   The implementation of the procedures is as follows:

```
constructor TDatabaseEvents.Create;
var
  statement: IDBStatement;
  objManager: TObjectManager;
  sqlScript: string;
begin
  inherited;
  fInsertedProc:= procedure (Args: TInsertedArgs)
                  begin
                    if Args.Entity is TAgent then
                    begin
                      statement:=(Args.Manager as
                      TObjectManager).Connection.
                      CreateStatement;
                      sqlScript:='update Base set CreateTS = '+
                              Double(Now).ToString+' where ID = '+
                                QuotedStr(TAgent(Args.Entity).
                                ID.ToString);
                        statement.SetSQLCommand(sqlScript);
                        statement.Execute;
                    end;
                  end;
```

```
fUpdatedProc:= procedure (Args: TUpdatedArgs)
              begin
                if Args.Entity is TAgent then
                begin
                  statement:=(Args.Manager as
                  TObjectManager).Connection.CreateStatement;
                  sqlScript:='update Base set ModifyTS = '+
                        Double(Now).ToString+' where ID = '+
                          QuotedStr(TAgent(Args.Entity).
                          ID.ToString);
                    statement.SetSQLCommand(sqlScript);
                    statement.Execute;
                end;
              end;
end;
```

3. In this approach, we use direct SQL calls to modify the properties. We build an update SQL query and execute it in the same way we did when we managed the definition of the view we used in the previous chapter.

    In order to execute the SQL query, we need access to the associated object manager. TInsertedArgs. Manager provides the right instance of it (note the need to cast this property to get access to the object manager).

    You may wonder why we did not use the usual approach of instantiating an IDatabaseSession and use a typical TObjectManager.Save to update the entity. What stops us from this is the fact that the OnInserted event is triggered before the insert transaction is fully completed and released. This means that the database is locked to the specific entity we are trying to modify in the event. Therefore, this approach is unusable.

Additionally, even if we were able to bypass the database locking, a call to Save from within the event would generate subsequent calls to the same event leading to a repetitive loop of Save and OnInserted calls.

TAureliusDataSet

Note   The code in this section requires the TeeChart TDBChart, which is not part of the standard TeeChart package that comes with Delphi. You need to visit TeeChart's web site, download and install the trial version (FMX component) if you want to run the code files.

Aurelius provides a dataset descendant (TAureliusDataSet) to facilitate data binding with visual controls (data-aware). It is cross-platform and, because it is based on Delphi's own TDataSet component, it can be used to link to any controls that employ TDataSet's functionality. If you need to look at the details, please visit the technical manual. You will be able to find up-to-date information.

The dashboard tab in CallCentre includes two graphs we need to populate. These graphs are based on TeeChart library which introduces the TChart and TDBChart components. In this section, we are going to use TAureliusDataSet to retrieve data in two different ways: one via the use of criteria-based query and one via the implementation of a view. You can find the full project in the *Call Centre – TAureliusDataSet* folder in the code file. Please, also, note that in this project I have replaced the TChart with a TDBChart to take advantage of the data set functionality.

1. Open the CallCentre project, drop two TAureliusDataSet components from the tool palette, and name them as adsAbandonRate and adsSatisfaction (Figure 6-3).

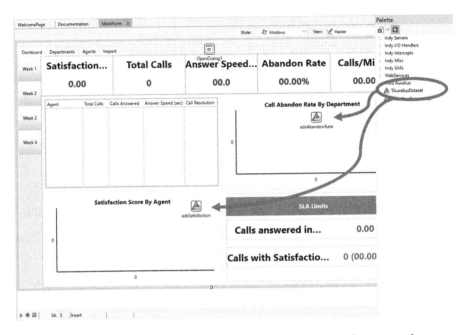

Figure 6-3. *The TAureliusDataSet components in the main form*

2. Add a new private method updateCharts in the MainForm. We will use this method to generate the data for the charts. For now, it is empty; we will populate it in the next steps. Add a call to the method in updateDashboard.

190

```
...
interface
type
  TFormMain = class(TForm)
  ...
  private
    ...
    procedure updateCharts (const aWeek: TWeeks);
  public
    ...
  end;
...
implementation
...
procedure TFormMain.updateCharts(const aWeek: TWeeks);
begin
  // We are going to fill this in in the next parts
end;

procedure TFormMain.updateDashboard(const aWeek: TWeeks);
begin
  ...
  updateCharts(aWeek);
end;
```

Criteria-Based Data Set

The adsSatisfaction data set retrieves data from the database about the satisfaction score of each agent. Locate updateCharts and add the following code:

```pascal
procedure TFormMain.updateCharts(const aWeek: TWeeks);
var
  session: IDatabaseSession;
  criteriaAgents: TCriteria;
begin
  adsSatisfaction.Close;

  session:=TDatabaseSession.Create(SQLiteConnection.
CreateConnection);

  criteriaAgents:=session.objectManager.Find<TCall>
                              .CreateAlias('AgentID', 'agent')
                                .Select(TProjections.
                                ProjectionList
                                  .Add(TProjections.Avg(Linq
                                  ['SatisfactionScore']).
                                  As_('SatisfactionScore'))
                                  .Add(TProjections.
                                  Prop('agent.Description').
                                  As_('Agent'))
                                  .Add(TProjections.Group
                                  ('agent.Description'))
                                )
                                .OrderBy('agent.Description');

  criteriaAgents:=filter(aWeek, criteriaAgents);

  adsSatisfaction.SetSourceCriteria(criteriaAgents);
  adsSatisfaction.Open;

  BarSeries1.DataSource:=adsSatisfaction;
  BarSeries1.YValues.ValueSource:='SatisfactionScore';
  BarSeries1.XLabelsSource:='Agent';
end;
```

As you can observe, we are not doing anything sophisticated. We create a new instance of the IDatabaseSession and initialize it as we have done many times already. Then, we construct the query based on TCriteria. We have done this as well before. The only new twist here is that we pass the criteria directly to TAureliusDataSet by, simply, calling SetSourceCriteria.

View-Based Data Set

For the second chart, we are going to use a view to demonstrate the flexibility of TAureliusDataSet. First, let's create the view; we need the abandon rate grouped by department. Because of the way we have designed CallCentre project, we, also, need it grouped by week.

We already know how to create a View; go to createViews procedure in MainForm.pas and add the following lines. You can find the SQL script in the code files in the *Misc* folder (AbandonRatePerDepartment.sql).

```
procedure TFormMain.createViews(const dbSession:
IDatabaseSession);
...
begin
  ...
  sqlScript:=
  'CREATE VIEW IF NOT EXISTS AbandonRatePerDepartment AS
  Select'+
  '  Call.ID,'+
  '  Week,'+
  '  Department.Description,'+
  '  (Count( case'+
  '    when QueueExitTime is null then 1'+
  '  end ) * 100.0 ) / count(*) as AbandonRate '+
  'FROM'+
```

```
  '  Call '+
  'INNER JOIN'+
  '  Department '+
  'ON Call.DepartmentID = Department.ID '+
  'GROUP BY'+
  '  Week,'+
  '  Department.ID '+
  'ORDER BY'+
  '  Week,'+
  '  Department.Description;';

  statement.SetSQLCommand(sqlScript);
  statement.Execute;
end;
```

In order to demonstrate different ways to link to TAureliusDataSet, we are going to create a TList to hold the results of the preceding view. Back in updateCharts, add the following code:

```
procedure TFormMain.updateCharts(const aWeek: TWeeks);
var
  ...,
  rateList: TList<TAbandonRatePerDepartment>;
begin
  ...
  adsAbandonRate.Close;

  criteriaDepartments:=session.objectManager('Database').Find<T
  AbandonRatePerDepartment>;
  criteriaDepartments:=filter(aWeek, criteriaDepartments);

  rateList:=criteriaDepartments.List<TAbandonRatePerDepartment>;
```

```
adsAbandonRate.SetSourceList(rateList);
adsAbandonRate.Open;

HorizBarSeries1.DataSource:=adsAbandonRate;
HorizBarSeries1.YValues.ValueSource:='AbandonRate';
HorizBarSeries1.XLabelsSource:='Description';

  rateList.Free;
end;
```

In this case, we use SetSourceList to pass data to TAureliusDataSet. The way we build rateList is familiar and consistent with what we have done up to this point. Note that in this case we need to explicitly free rateList; otherwise we will induce memory leaks. However, we do not have to do the same with TCriteria as it is intrinsically managed by the data set.

Summary

In this chapter, we looked at how object-oriented methodologies blend with the functionality of Aurelius as an ORM framework. The inheritance property of objects and the events provide opportunities to automate processes and expand functionality. In addition, this chapter demonstrated how we can use a graphical component (TAureliusDataSet) to pass information to third-party data-aware components.

CHAPTER 7

Aurelius on the Move

It is common to use an ORM system to support desktop applications or
the back end of servers. This is exactly what we have done so far. We have
developed a FireMonkey desktop application and used Aurelius to access a
local database storage.

In this chapter, we take the task of moving Aurelius to mobile
platforms. You can use any kind of such platforms, be it mobile phones or
tablets. In the projects we work on in this part of the book, I use an Android
tablet running Android 7.0 Nougat.

Data Accessibility

In the first chapter, we discussed how ORM frameworks fit in three-tier
applications (Figure 7-1). The `CallCentre` application we have been
working on all this time does not explicitly treat those layers separately
as we wanted to focus on Aurelius' features. When you move to mobile
applications (not web applications that can be accessed via browsers), the
need to separate the concerns becomes more prominent as availability of
resources such as storage and computational power may be in inadequacy.

Broadly speaking, when it comes to utilizing a database, there are two
approaches you can take:

- **Use a local database**: This can be a database file as
  the one we use in our application or a database server
  running on the mobile (e.g., Berkeley DB, Couchbase
  Lite, SQLite Server).

© John Kouraklis 2019
J. Kouraklis, *Introducing Delphi ORM*, https://doi.org/10.1007/978-1-4842-5013-6_7

- **Use a remote server–based database**: In this
  approach, the database is stored in a server in a remote
  location, and the mobile application sends queries to
  the server. This is usually implemented as REST client-
  server architecture, and the exchange of data conforms
  to predefined protocols (JSON, XML).

Aurelius can fit in all the preceding scenarios. In fact, once you use
the framework, it is not difficult to switch between different designs or,
even better, to use a combination of them; for example, you can use a local
database to store some user-specific data and connect to a server for the
main data sets.

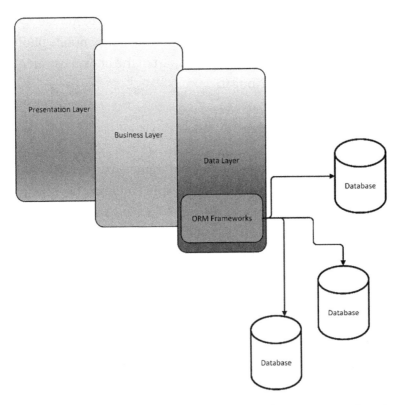

Figure 7-1. *The role of ORM frameworks in three-tier applications*
(reproduced from Chapter 1)

Local Database

Moving CallCentre to an Android installation with a local database is not very hard to do. Our mobile solution implements the arrangement in Figure 7-1 as an application that incorporates all the layers and uses a local SQLite database. The full Delphi project can be found in the *Call Centre – Local* folder in the code of this chapter, and you can find a project to start working on your own in the *Call Centre* folder.

Our project is a FireMonkey application and, therefore, you should be able to build it for Android and execute it. From the perspective of Aurelius, we need to make a small adjustment. When we configured the TAureliusConnection in ConnectionModule.pas, we hardcoded the location and the name of the database file by adding the value of ".\database.db" in the Database field in the wizard of the connection.

On Windows, this means that the database file is created in the same directory as the executable (binary) file. On Android, there is a different policy in place and applications can write files only in very special locations managed by the operating system. In practice, this means that the path we have will not work, and in fact if you run the project you will see that it crashes when launched.

In order to fix this issue, we are going to ask the operating system to provide the appropriate location. Delphi provides many ways to do this; the simplest is to use the GetDocumentsPath function. The modification is as follows in TSQLiteConnection.CreateConnection function. As you can observe, I use the ANDROID conditional compiler directive to isolate the code.

```
unit ConnectionModule;

interface
...
implementation
...
uses
```

```
...,
System.IOUtils;

class function TSQLiteConnection.CreateConnection:
IDBConnection;
begin
{$IFDEF ANDROID}
  SQLiteConnection.AureliusConnection1.Params.
  Values['Database']:=
      TPath.Combine(TPath.GetDocumentsPath, 'database.db');
{$ENDIF}
  Result := SQLiteConnection.AureliusConnection1.
  CreateConnection;
end;
```

Figure 7-2 shows a screenshot of the CallCentre application on Android.

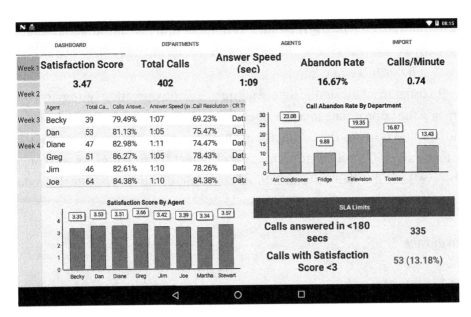

Figure 7-2. *The* CallCentre *application on Android tablet*

Note   There are a few more changes that had to be done to make
CallCentre run on Android, but I skip them, as they are not Aurelius
related. To provide a guidance if you want to explore the code more,
look at the changes in FrameImportbtImportClick event in
MainForm.pas, the FileSelectForm.pas (which provides a
simple replacement of TOpenDialog for Android), the importData
method in Database.Import.pas, and the deployment of assets
(Deployment Manager).

Remote Server–Based Database

A database can be hosted in a remote location accessible via HTTP
protocols. In such cases, a remote server feeds data to the client
applications using well-defined exchange rules and formats (distributed
applications). Moreover, the server, most of the times, incorporates a large
amount (if not all) of the business logic to lighten the work that needs to be
done in the client application (Figure 7-3).

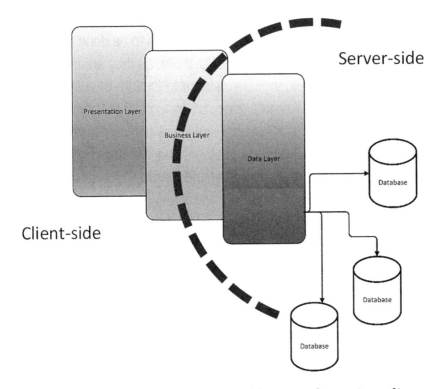

Figure 7-3. *Separation of the data and business layers in a client-server arrangement*

Aurelius, as an ORM framework, facilitates the access to the underlying databases. In a server-client design, there are more than one ways to utilize its capabilities. In Figure 7-4 you can see that the framework can fit in either the client or the server side.

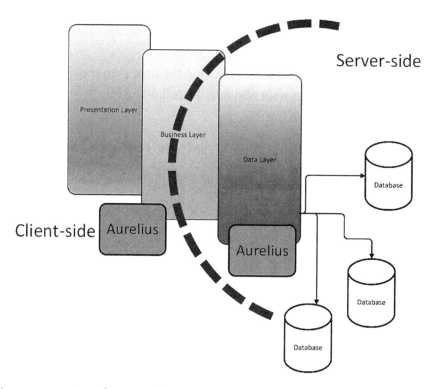

Figure 7-4. *Aurelius can fit in both client and server sides of distributed applications*

Client Side

When we look at a client application, which fetches data from a database, we are essentially dealing with exchange of data in a way that the client understands. Servers use JSON as the preferred (but not as the only) format to send data over the Internet, and our ORM framework needs to be able to decipher a JSON file and produce the required entities.

In order to demonstrate how Aurelius framework can assist in this direction, we are going to use a sample data set from JSONPlaceholder (2019) web site. JSONPlaceholder provides fake data sets accessible via a RESTful API. At the time of writing, the data sets include data for posts, comments, and users. There are, also, data sets for albums and to-do lists but we will not use them.

1. We are going to start by accessing the user with the ID 1. Open a browser and add the following line in the web address bar:

    `https://jsonplaceholder.typicode.com/users/1`

    JSONPlaceholder will respond with a JSON file like the one in Figure 7-5.

Figure 7-5. *JSON response for a user from JSONPlaceholder web site*

2. The response reveals three JSON objects: the *user*
    itself, the *address,* and the *company.* Moreover,
    address object has a *geo* object with geographical
    coordinates.

3. Create a new console project and add a new unit
    under the name Entities.pas. If you wish to see
    the full project, check the *User* folder in the code
    files of this chapter.

4. In Entities.pas, add the following code:

```
interface

uses
  SysUtils,
  Generics.Collections,
  Aurelius.Mapping.Attributes,
  Aurelius.Types.DynamicProperties;

type
  TAddress = class;
  TCompany = class;
  TGeolocation = class;
  TUsers = class;

  [Entity]
  [Table('Address')]
  [Id('Fid', TIdGenerator.None)]
  TAddress = class
  private
    [Column('id', [TColumnProp.Required])]
    Fid: Integer;

    [Column('street', [], 255)]
    Fstreet: string;
```

```
    [Column('suite', [], 255)]
    Fsuite: string;

    [Column('city', [], 255)]
    Fcity: string;

    [Column('zipcode', [], 255)]
    Fzipcode: string;

    [Association([], CascadeTypeAll - [TCascadeType.Remove])]
    [JoinColumn('geo', [], 'id')]
    Fgeo: TGeolocation;
  public
    property id: Integer read Fid write Fid;
    property street: string read Fstreet write Fstreet;
    property suite: string read Fsuite write Fsuite;
    property city: string read Fcity write Fcity;
    property zipcode: string read Fzipcode write Fzipcode;
    property geo: TGeolocation read Fgeo write Fgeo;
  end;

  [Entity]
  [Table('Company')]
  [Id('Fid', TIdGenerator.None)]
  TCompany = class
  private
    [Column('id', [TColumnProp.Required])]
    Fid: Integer;

    [Column('name', [], 255)]
    Fname: string;

    [Column('catchPhrase', [], 255)]
    F???catchPhrase: string;
```

```
  [Column('bs', [], 255)]
  Fbs: string;
public
  property id: Integer read Fid write Fid;
  property name: string read Fname write Fname;
  property catchPhrase: string read FcatchPhrase write
  FcatchPhrase;
  property bs: string read Fbs write Fbs;
end;

[Entity]
[Table('Geolocation')]
[Id('Fid', TIdGenerator.None)]
TGeolocation = class
private
  [Column('id', [TColumnProp.Required])]
  Fid: Integer;

  [Column('lat', [], 255)]
  Flat: string;

  [Column('lng', [], 255]
  Flng: string;
public
  property id: Integer read Fid write Fid;
  property lat: string read Flat write Flat;
  property lng: string read Flng write Flng;
end;

[Entity]
[Table('Users')]
[Id('Fid', TIdGenerator.None)]
TUsers = class
```

```
private
  [Column('id', [TColumnProp.Required])]
  Fid: Integer;

  [Column('name', [], 255)]
  Fname: string;

  [Column('username', [], 255)]
  Fusername: string;

  [Column('email', [], 255)]
  Femail: string;

  [Column('phone', [], 255)]
  Fphone: string;

  [Column('website', [], 255)]
  Fwebsite: string;

  [Association([], CascadeTypeAll - [TCascadeType.Remove])]
  [JoinColumn('company', [], 'id')]
  Fcompany: TCompany;

  [Association([], CascadeTypeAll - [TCascadeType.Remove])]
  [JoinColumn('address', [], 'id')]
  Faddress: TAddress;
public
  property id: Integer read Fid write Fid;
  property name: string read Fname write Fname;
  property username: string read Fusername write Fusername;
  property email: string read Femail write Femail;
  property phone: string read Fphone write Fphone;
  property website: string read Fwebsite write Fwebsite;
  property company: TCompany read Fcompany write Fcompany;
  property address: TAddress read Faddress write Faddress;
end;
```

```
implementation

initialization
  RegisterEntity(TGeolocation);
  RegisterEntity(TAddress);
  RegisterEntity(TUsers);
  RegisterEntity(TCompany);

finalization

end.
```

In the preceding code, you can see familiar elements and there is nothing new, actually. The reason I include the full unit is to emphasize a few points in relation to the original JSON file the Placeholder site generated.

a. The mapped members must have the exact case as they appear in the JSON file. The corresponding properties, though, can have a different case.

b. The linked (associated) entities should not be declared as Lazy. The information in the JSON file as supplied by the web site is not enough for Aurelius to manage lazy loading.

c. Nullable<T> data types should not be declared. This means all properties should be mandatory at database level.

5. Add the following code to retrieve the JSON file from the web site:

```
...
uses
  System.SysUtils,
  IdHTTP;
```

```
var
  idHTTP: TIdHTTP;
  response: string;
begin
  try
    idHTTP:=TIdHTTP.Create(nil);
    response:=idHTTP.Get('http://jsonplaceholder.typicode.com/
    users/1');
    idHTTP.Free;
  except
    ...
  end;
end.
```

If you debug the code, you will see that response
gets the full JSON file. Additionally, as a quick note,
I use the http protocol rather than the https to
simplify the use of TIdHTTP component.

6. Now, let us reconstruct the user entity. In order to
do this, we need help from Aurelius. The framework
provides a helper class in BCL.JSON unit, which is
capable of serializing and deserializing objects in
JSON format. The helper function uses generics to
infer the properties of an object and then produces
a string with the JSON representation. The usage is
straightforward.

```
...
uses
  System.SysUtils,
  IdHTTP,
  Entities in 'Entities.pas',
  Bcl.Json;

var
  ...,
  newUser: TUsers;

begin
  try
    ...
    newUser:=TJSON.Deserialize<TUsers>(response);
    newUser.Free;
    idHTTP.Free;
  except
    ...
  end;
end.
```

newUser holds now all the values from the JSON
response. Aurelius created a new instance of TUsers
as you can observe if you set a breakpoint and see
the object in the debugger (Figure 7-6). At this stage,
we've got an entity that can be managed in isolation
or in a fresh Aurelius database virtual system.

Watch List - Thread 7312	﹖ ✕
Watch Name	**Value**
⌄ ☑ newUser	(1, 'Leanne Graham', 'Bret', '...
Fid	1
Fname	'Leanne Graham'
Fusername	'Bret'
Femail	'Sincere@april.biz'
Fphone	'1-770-736-8031 x56442'
Fwebsite	'hildegard.org'
⌄ Fcompany	$2E5C4C0
Fid	0
Fname	'Romaguera-Crona'
FcatchPhrase	'Multi-layered client-server ...
Fbs	'harness real-time e-markets'
⌄ Faddress	$2E795C0
Fid	0
Fstreet	'Kulas Light'
Fsuite	'Apt. 556'
Fcity	'Gwenborough'
Fzipcode	'92998-3874'
⌄ Fgeo	$2E62980
Fid	0
Flat	'-37.3159'
Flng	'81.1496'
Watches	

Figure 7-6. *A new instance of JSON-created TUser object*

7. The last thing we do is to free the newUser instance. However, if you run the code and check for memory leaks, you will see there are some bytes we have not cleaned up. The reason is that TUser links to two other objects (TAddress and TCompany) and TAddress to another one (TGeolocation). We have to explicitly free them too.

```
begin
  try
    ...
    newUser:=TJSON.Deserialize<TUsers>(response);
    newUser.address.geo.Free;
    newUser.address.Free;
    newUser.company.Free;
    newUser.Free;

    idHTTP.Free;
  except
    ...
  end;
end.
```

This demonstrates how easy it is to manipulate JSON files from external and third-party APIs. If you want to see how you can retrieve lists of objects from JSONPlaceholder, have a look at the *Client* folder in the code files of this chapter (AureliusClient project), which can run on multiple platforms (Figure 7-7).

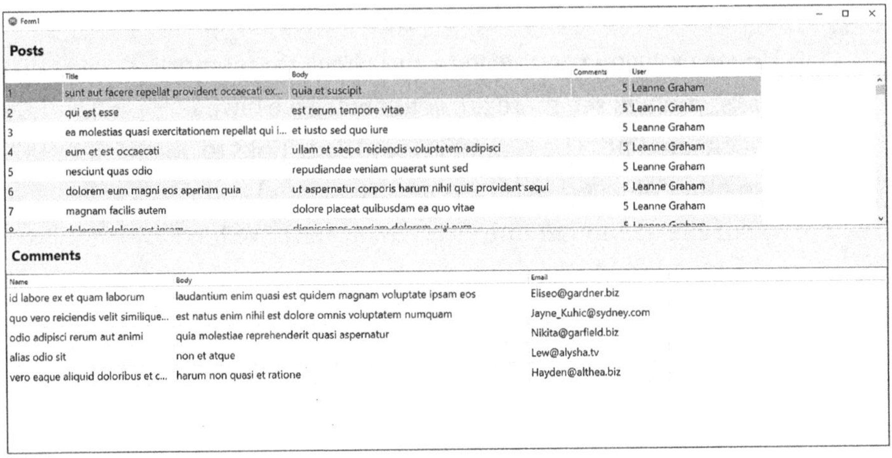

Figure 7-7. *Aurelius deserialization of JSON files using JSONPlaceholder's API*

Server Side

Serving a REST server that uses Aurelius is similar to what we did in the previous section but in the opposite fashion. Instead of deserializing an object, we just serialize it to a JSON string.

...

```
serialisedUser:=TJSON.SerializeAs<TUsers>(newUser);
```

...

XData

The previous examples demonstrate how to manage rather arbitrary JSON data structures, meaning that the structure of the generated JSON file does not adhere to any rules and it is really a matter of decisions made by the developers of JSONPlaceholder.

This may not pose a problem if the scale of the projects you are involved in is not big, but in general it is safer to use more standardized approaches. Open Data Protocol (OData, 2019) is a set of rules to build RESTful APIs, and a big part of it involves the definition of appropriate JSON file structure. TMS provides TMS XDATA, a product inspired by OData and smoothly integrated with Aurelius.

Aurelius is, deeply, intertwined with XData; and, this gives the advantage of generating, very quickly and efficiently, a server-client solution backed by a database. As a case, we are going to create a server that exposes the database and the entities from our `CallCentre` project and a client that retrieves the agents' data. You can find the projects of this part in the *XData* folder in the code files.

Note   The projects in this section require TMS XData. This is a separate product sold by TMS. You can download a trial version from the TMS product page.

The server is able to access the database entities via a typical Aurelius connection as we have configured and used in the previous chapters.

1. After you have XData installed in your Delphi environment, go to *File* ➤ *New* ➤ *Other...* ➤ *TMS XData* and select *TMS XData VCL Server* (Figure 7-8).

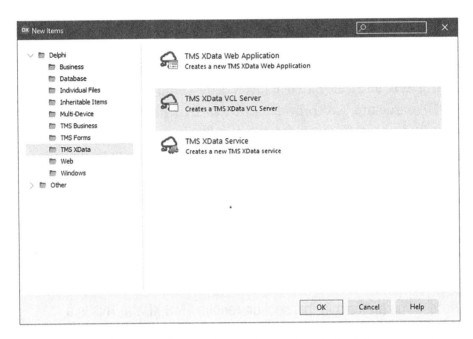

Figure 7-8. *Selecting XData wizard from the File ➤ New menu in Delphi*

That is pretty much what you have to do to create the server.

2. Go to Unit1.pas (or to Container.pas of the Server project in the *XData* folder) in the design mode and select the XDataServer component. In the object inspector, enter http://+:2001/callcenter in the BaseUrl field (Figure 7-9). This is the address we will use to access the database entities. In order for this to work correctly on Windows, the address needs to be registered with the operating system. If you want to see how to do this, please refer to the XData manual. Additionally, make sure you check the List and Get options in the DefaultEntitySetPermissions.

216

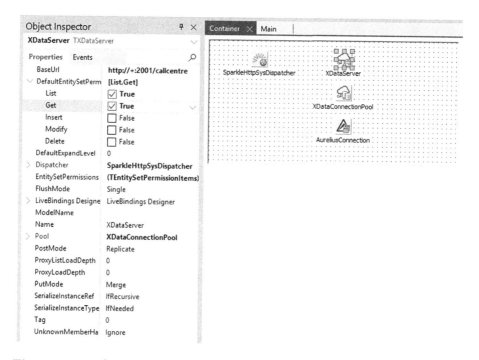

Figure 7-9. *The edited XDataServer properties*

3. Configure `AureliusConnection` to use a local `SQLite` database.

4. Add the `Entities.pas` file from our main `CallCentre` project.

5. Run the project and make sure the server is running.

6. Open a web browser.

7. Enter `http://localhost:2001/callcentre` in the address bar and hit `Enter`. You will be able to see the available *endpoints* the server has generated (Figure 7-10). As you can observe, they represent the entity names of our database design. Aurelius has supplied them to XData server.

217

```
localhost:2001/callcen  ×    +           —  □  ×

←  →  C      ⓘ  localhost:2001/callcentre      🖪  ⋮

{
    "value": [
        {
            "name": "Department",
            "url": "Department"
        },
        {
            "name": "Call",
            "url": "Call"
        },
        {
            "name": "Agent",
            "url": "Agent"
        },
        {
            "name": "Base",
            "url": "Base"
        }
    ]
}
```

Figure 7-10. *XData retrieves the entity structure from Aurelius and makes it accessible via an API*

8. Enter `http://localhost:2001/callcentre/Agent`
    in the address bar and hit `Enter`. Now we get a list of
    the agents (Figure 7-11). Aurelius has, successfully,
    fetched the data from the database and XData has
    exposed them in a JSON format.

```
  localhost:2001/callcentre/Agent  ×  +                              —   □   ×

←  →  C    ①  localhost:2001/callcentre/Agent                          🗐   ⋮

{
    "value": [
        {
            "$id": 1,
            "ID": "0427654E-A435-4B71-89A8-F1BAD80A154D",
            "CreateUser": "system",
            "CreateTS": "2019-05-07T00:29:42.344",
            "ModifyUser": null,
            "ModifyTS": null,
            "Description": "Jim",
            "Photo@xdata.proxy": "Agent(0427654E-A435-4B71-89A8-F1BAD80A154D)/Photo",
            "CallList@xdata.proxy": "Agent(0427654E-A435-4B71-89A8-F1BAD80A154D)/CallList"
        },
        {
            "$id": 2,
            "ID": "919FB89C-1FD0-461E-AB99-8EFBC53DA692",
            "CreateUser": "system",
            "CreateTS": "2019-05-07T00:29:42.669",
            "ModifyUser": null,
            "ModifyTS": null,
            "Description": "Stewart",
            "Photo@xdata.proxy": "Agent(919FB89C-1FD0-461E-AB99-8EFBC53DA692)/Photo",
            "CallList@xdata.proxy": "Agent(919FB89C-1FD0-461E-AB99-8EFBC53DA692)/CallList"
        },
        {
            "$id": 3,
            "ID": "F57339D7-A214-422C-A272-A24E6091A90C",
            "CreateUser": "system",
            "CreateTS": "2019-05-07T00:29:42.964",
            "ModifyUser": null,
            "ModifyTS": null,
            "Description": "Diane",
            "Photo@xdata.proxy": "Agent(F57339D7-A214-422C-A272-A24E6091A90C)/Photo",
            "CallList@xdata.proxy": "Agent(F57339D7-A214-422C-A272-A24E6091A90C)/CallList"
        },
        {
            "$id": 4,
            "ID": "4207599F-EEFC-49E8-830D-60C9D4D4C1F0",
            "CreateUser": "system",
```

Figure 7-11. *List of agents as generated by XData*

The involvement of Aurelius finishes at this stage. XData provides the TXDataClient component that can be used in a client application and makes the manipulation of JSON data as easy as when you deal with Aurelius directly. In fact, it exposes a fluent interface that assimilates the Aurelius methods.

Let us create a simple project to consume the data XData sends. You can find the complete project under the name Client in the *XData* folder.

1. We need a form to show the data we receive like in the Figure 7-12. There is no reason to go through the details here. You can find the form if you like in the code files.

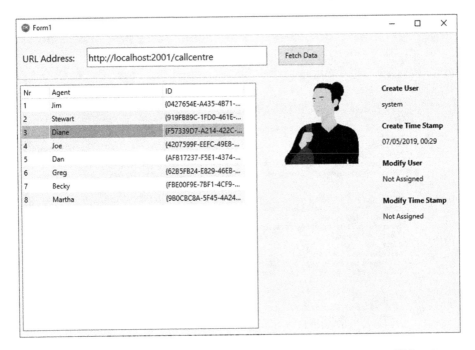

Figure 7-12.   Final form showing data retrieved via XDataClient

2. In the OnCreate and OnDestroy events of the button
    at the top of the form, add the following code to
    instantiate TXDataClient:

```
...
interface

type
  TForm1 = class(TForm)
    ...
    procedure FormDestroy(Sender: TObject);
    procedure FormCreate(Sender: TObject);
  private
    fClient: TXDataClient;
  public
```

```
    { Public declarations }
  end;
...
implementation

procedure TForm1.FormCreate(Sender: TObject);
begin
  fClient:=TXDataClient.Create;
end;

procedure TForm1.FormDestroy(Sender: TObject);
begin
  fClient.Free;
end;
```

3. In the OnClick event of the button at the top of the form, we pass the server address to the XDataClient and call loadAgents and, consequently, loadData. We also need to use the Database.Utilities unit.

```
type
  TForm1 = class(TForm)
    ...
    procedure btFetchClick(Sender: TObject);
  private
    ...
    procedure loadAgents;
    procedure loadData(const aGUID: string);
  public
    ...
  end;
...
implementation
```

```
uses
  ...,
  Database.Utilities;

procedure TFormMain.btFetchClick(Sender: TObject);
begin
  fClient.Uri:=edURL.Text;
  loadAgents;
end;

procedure TFormMain.loadAgents;
var
  list: TList<TAgent>;
  agent: TAgent;
begin
  ...
  list:=fClient.List<TAgent>;
  for agent in list do
  begin
    ...
  end;
  list.Free;
end;

procedure TFormMain.loadData(const aGUID: string);
var
  ...,
  agent: TAgent;
begin
  agent:=fClient.Get<TAgent, TGUID>(StringToGUID(aGUID));
  if Assigned(agent) then
```

```
begin
    ...
  end;
end;
```

I have omitted the code that updates the user interface for simplicity. The points to be noted refer to the highlighted parts in the preceding code. The code lines show how we can use XDataClient. A closer observation reveals that the format of the calls to generate the database entities from the JSON file is, exactly, the same as in Aurelius.

Summary

In this chapter, we considered how to move Aurelius to mobile platforms. There are some implications, and at the same time new opportunities arise. We moved the application we developed in the previous chapters to mobile platforms, and we explored how Aurelius can sit in either the client or the server side to serve different needs.

References

OData, 2019. Open Data Protocol. [Online] Available at: www.odata.org/ [Accessed 06 05 2019].

Placeholder, J., 2019. JSONPlaceholder. [Online] Available at: https:// jsonplaceholder.typicode.com/ [Accessed 05 05 2019].

CHAPTER 8

TMS Data Modeler

All the code we have developed up to this point centers on the code-first approach. This means that our database design is based on the needs we identify when we get our hands in the application design. As developers, we first consider the business side of an application and then we resolve to object-oriented patterns in order to build a software solution.

As discussed in Chapter 1, code-first approach is not the only available path developers can take. They can equally start from modeling the back end of the software solution they are designing (model-first) or, in the very real and common cases where software needs to be developed on existing databases, they look at the database first and construct the application to fit in the database (database-first pattern).

The Application

Aurelius, as we have seen, makes code-first design a breeze. For the other approaches, we turn our focus to TMS Data Modeler. Data Modeler is a proprietary application developed and maintained by TMS Software and comes as a separate product. It provides a flexible and easy way to manage both model-first and database-first designs. In the next sections, we explore the two approaches using the `CallCentre` project. There is a wealth of features in the application, and you can find more details in the technical manual that accompanies the product.

© John Kouraklis 2019
J. Kouraklis, *Introducing Delphi ORM*, https://doi.org/10.1007/978-1-4842-5013-6_8

For our examples, there are three points to look at:

- **Diagram (Model) Editor**: This is accessible from the left-side panel and provides a graphical representation of the entities and the tables in a database (Figure 8-1). Data Modeler organizes graphs of entities into diagrams.

- **Importing of existing databases**: In the cases where an existing database is being inherited to the project, you can import the database schema and allow Data Modeler generate the tables and the entities automatically.

- **Export to Aurelius entities**: This is perhaps the most valuable feature of Data Modeler. Once the entities have been defined, Data Modeler can generate a Delphi unit with the declarations of the classes you need for Aurelius.

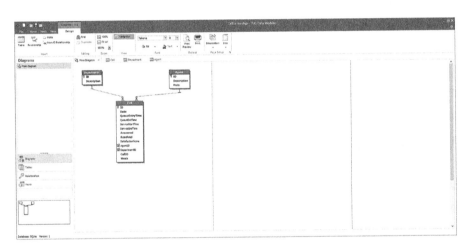

Figure 8-1. *The Data Modeler application (diagrams)*

Note   The examples in this chapter require the Data Modeler application which is a separate product sold by TMS Software. Please check the product page in the company's web site.

Model-First

In this approach, developers work at a conceptual level. They are not concerned with the database specificities and focus on implementing entity designs to support the business value and challenges of the applications they are developing. Let's move on and create a model for our CallCentre project. You can find the full Data Modeler project in the files that come with this book (CallCentre.dgp).

1. Create a new project in Data Modeler by selecting the *File* ➤ *New* ➤ *New Project* menu.

2. In the next dialog box, select SQLite as the database of our preference (Figure 8-2). This is the database engine we use in our examples, but in case you want to change to something else Data Modeler allows you to migrate a project from one database to another.

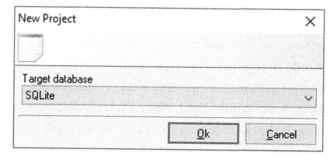

Figure 8-2. *Target database dialog when a new project is generated*

3. Select *Diagrams* from the left-sidebar and you will see a diagram already created (Main Diagram). Select the *Design* tab in the Ribbon and click *Table* item (Figure 8-3). After you select the button in the Ribbon, you need to click the white space in the Main Diagram tab to see the details of the table.

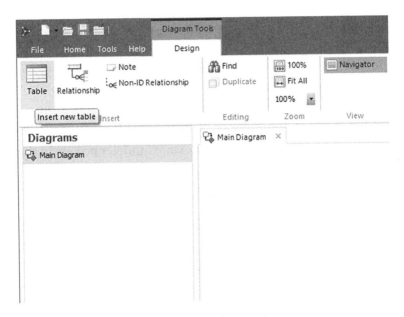

Figure 8-3. *Inserting a new table in the project*

4. Add the details of the Department entity as seen in
    Figure 8-4. Two fields worth mentioning in this form
    are the *Logic Type* and the *Physical Type* fields. You
    can only change the logic type of a field in an entity.
    This is where you declare what kind of data you are
    expecting the field to hold. Then, Data Modeler works
    out the actual field type in the database. It is able to do
    this because when we created the project we declared
    SQLite as the underlying database engine.

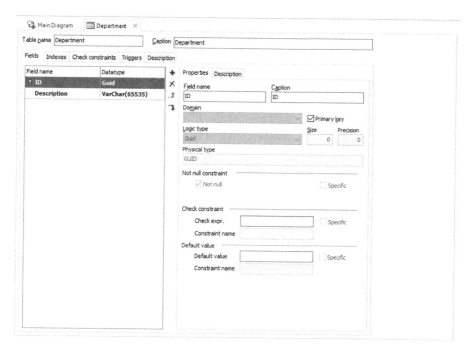

Figure 8-4. *The details of Department entity*

5. Create the entities for Agent and Call as in
    Figures 8-5 and 8-6.

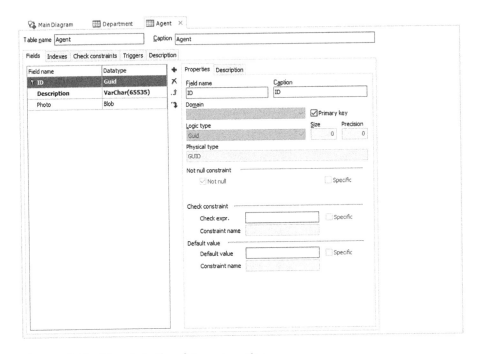

Figure 8-5. *The details of Agent entity*

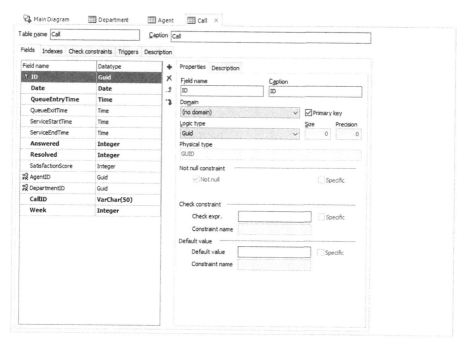

Figure 8-6. *The details of Call entity*

6. At this stage, we have the entities in our model.
   The next step is to create the associations between
   them. In Call entity, there is the DepartmentID
   field that represents the foreign key to the ID field
   in Department entity. Go back to the *Main Diagram*
   and select the *Non-ID Relationship* from the Ribbon
   (*Design* tab) as in Figure 8-7. Non-ID relationship in
   Aurelius is an association between two entities where
   the foreign key is not part of the primary key; for
   example, if we had a compound primary key in Call
   comprising the department (e.g., 1-Air Condition),
   then we would have to link Department and Call via
   a normal relationship and not a non-ID relationship.
   The latter type is the most commonly used.

231

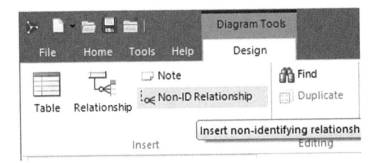

Figure 8-7. *Inserting a non-ID relationship*

Using the mouse, drag a line from *Department* to *Call.*
This will open the Relationship Editor (Figure 8-8).
Click the Child Table ID field and you will be able to
select a different value. This is not very obvious in the
user interface; you may need to double-click the ID
field. Select DepartmentID as the foreign key in *Call.*
In the same form, you can adjust how you want the
relationship to behave in the case of a deletion or
update of a *Department.* Then click OK.

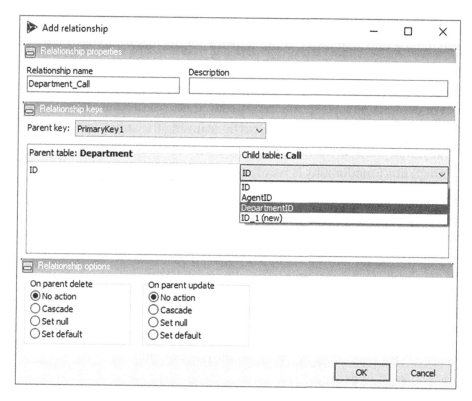

Figure 8-8. *The Relationship Editor*

7. In a similar way, add a relationship between Agent and Call.

At this stage, you should have all the entities defined and the relationship declared. The main diagram should look like the one in Figure 8-1.

Database-First

The other approach to work with databases and ORM frameworks is to start from a database. This means that you or someone else has already created the tables, the field, and all the associations the database (and

233

the applications that use it) needs. It is very handy to be able to inspect the database and, somehow, regenerate the model of the database and, consequently, the entities in our ORM. We can achieve this in Data Modeler via the reverse engineering feature.

For completeness, it should be noted that `TAureliusConnection` allows the generation of entity classes by scanning the attached database directly from the IDE. This is a shortcut to the database-first approach. Although this functionality is very handy, it does not allow any level of customization. On the other hand, Data Modeler offers a wealth of options.

In order to demonstrate how it works, we are going to use a database from the previous chapters. You can generate the database running one of the projects we developed in Chapter 7.

1. Create a new project in Data Modeler by selecting the *File* ➤ *New* ➤ *Import from Database* menu.

2. In the wizard, create a new SQLite connection (Figure 8-9) and then locate the database file (Figure 8-10).

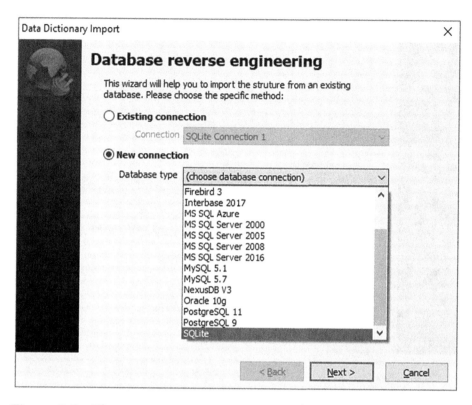

Figure 8-9. *The reverse engineering wizard (new connection)*

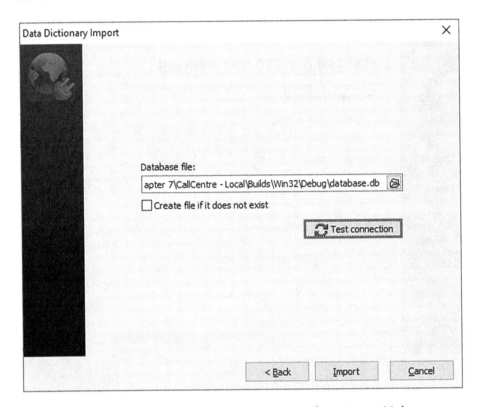

Figure 8-10. *The reverse engineering wizard (database file)*

3. Select *Import* and complete the wizard. Now, you have the model based on the database file and you are able to do any amendments you wish.

Export to Aurelius

In the previous sections, we created a model from scratch without getting into any details from any database, and we imported the scheme from a database and generated the corresponding model. The next step is to link back to the ORM framework.

Data Modeler provides the ability to export the model to Aurelius. It is one of the most valuable features in my view as it removes the need to write code manually. You can create one or more units with entities, fields, properties, and associations very easily which increases productivity a lot. You may wish to do some adjustments, but it can save you a lot of time and effort, especially if you are dealing with massive databases.

Entities

It is very easy to create a unit with all the entities in your database. Here we are going to create the basic entities we used in the CallCentre project.

1. Go to *Tools* tab in the Ribbon and select *TMS Aurelius* (Figure 8-11).

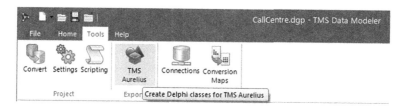

Figure 8-11. *The TMS Aurelius export option in Data Modeler*

2. The following form is revealed (Figure 8-12).

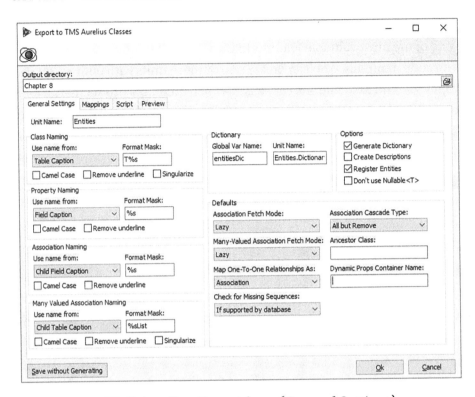

Figure 8-12. *TMS Aurelius Export form (General Settings)*

3. Click the Mappings tab and keep the Agent, Call, and Department entities checked. This tells the wizard to generate Aurelius code for these entities only (Figure 8-13).

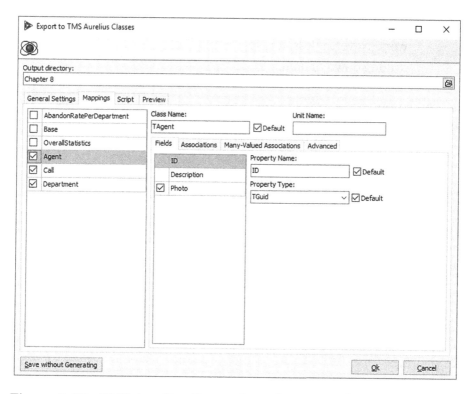

Figure 8-13. *TMS Aurelius Export form (Mappings)*

The options in the form are self-explanatory. You have the ability to affect the generated code by modifying the name of the properties or the data type itself and preview the associations by switching to the *Associations* tab.

4. Switch to the *Many-Valued Associations* tab (Figure 8-14). If you have the Agent entity selected, you will see that the wizard can generate a list which links back to the associated endpoint (Call). This is something we added manually when we were exploring the many-valued associations, and the

239

lists are not compulsory for the ORM framework to work. Nevertheless, it is very helpful as it allows the drilling down of data.

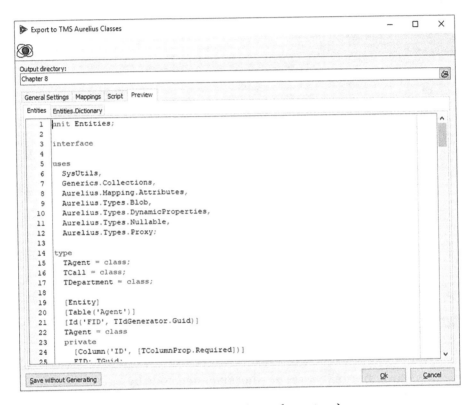

Figure 8-14. *TMS Aurelius Export form (Preview)*

5. Before the wizard exports the Aurelius entities, you can see the generated code if you go to the *Preview* tab (Figure 8-15). You are not able to modify the code here but only to observe what the wizard will generate. If you wish to add or remove entities, go back to the *Mappings* tab, make your changes and the code will be updated.

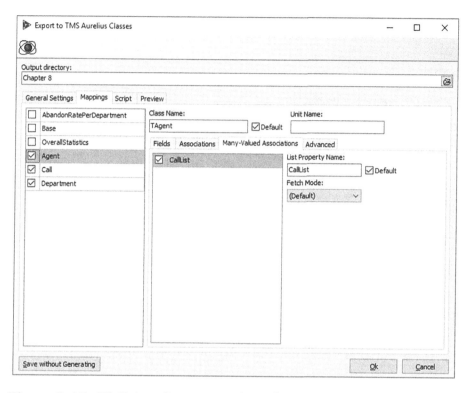

Figure 8-15. *TMS Aurelius Export form (Mappings/Many-Valued Associations)*

Dictionary

In *General Settings* tab in the *Export* wizard, there is a set of options that determine the creation of a property dictionary (Figure 8-16). These options can be confusing as most of the Delphi developers are familiar with the TDictionary class and they expect to see something that uses it.

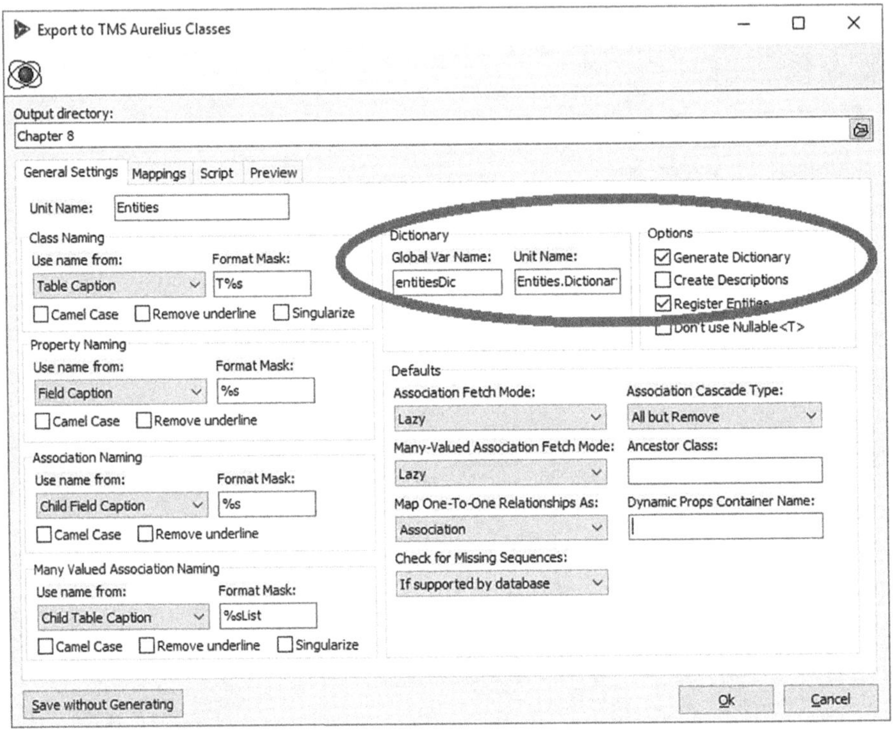

Figure 8-16. *Dictionary options in TMS Aurelius Export form*

What this *dictionary* is in the context of the Data Modeler and Aurelius is a convenient mapping of the properties in the entities to equivalent fields in classes. In this way, instead of referring to the properties in queries and projections by entering hardcoded strings, you can use class properties.

For example, in CallCentre project, we have the function filter, which adds a filter to queries.

```
...
function TFormMain.filter(const aWeek: TWeeks; const aCriteria:
TCriteria):
    TCriteria;
begin
```

```
  if aWeek = wWeek4   then
    result:= aCriteria.Add(Linq['Week'] >= 4)
  else
    result:= aCriteria.Add(Linq['Week'] = integer(aWeek)+1);
end;
```

Using the dictionary, we can make the following adjustment to the function:

```
...
uses
  ...,
  Entities.Dictionary;
...
function TFormMain.filter(const aWeek: TWeeks; const aCriteria:
TCriteria):
    TCriteria;
begin
  if aWeek = wWeek4   then
    result:=aCriteria.Add(Linq[entitiesDic.Call.Week.PropName]
    > = 4)
  else
    result:= aCriteria.Add(Linq[entitiesDic.Call.Week.PropName]
    = integer(aWeek)+1);
end;
```

The benefit we get from this approach is that we no longer worry about making any mistakes when we enter entity properties. Instead, we rely to the entitiesDic to provide the right property name. The downside is that the code may be seen as more convoluted as there are multiple references to a chain of properties. It is, really, on you to see whether and how this can fit in your coding style.

Events

The Aurelius unit the Data Modeler creates can be, directly, used to your applications. There are, however, occasions where some fine-tuning of the code is required. One such occasion is the inheritance strategy we followed when we wanted to introduce the create and modify details in the agent entries. This modification cannot be achieved using the export wizard.

Instead, we need to use another mechanism that is provided by Data Modeler. The application introduces a number of events triggered during the generation of the Aurelius source code. More specifically, at the time of writing, the following events are generated:

- When a unit is fully created (`OnUnitGenerated`)

- When a class (entity) is completely created (`OnClassGenerated`)

- When a property and the corresponding field are created in a class (`OnColumnGenerated`)

- When an association is created (`OnAssociationGenerated`)

- When a many-valued association is created (`OnManyValuedAssociationGenerated`)

You can find the full details for the events in the manual of Data Modeler. For our inheritance case, we will focus on the `OnClassGenerated` event. If we refer back to the modifications we did in our code to introduce and configure inheritance, we see that we added and removed some code from the `TBase` and `TAgent` classes.

In TBase class, we, only, added the inheritance attribute. Let us do this in Data Modeler.

1.   Launch the Aurelius Export wizard and make sure that the *Base* entity is selected in the *Mappings* tab (Figure 8-15). You can click the *Preview* tab and make sure code for TBase appears.

2.   Switch to the *Script* tab and click *Declare Events* button. You should be able to see all the events the wizard supports. We need the OnClassGenerated, so you can delete the rest to keep the script simple.

3.   Add the following code:

```
procedure OnClassGenerated(Args: TClassGeneratedArgs);
begin
  if Args.CodeType.Name = 'TBase' then
  begin
    Args.CodeType.AddAttribute('Inheritance').
                        AddRawArgument('TInheritance
                        Strategy.JoinedTables');
  end;
end;
```

4.   You can check that the attribute has been added in TBase entity if you go to the *Preview* tab.

Tip   If you want to check the properties and methods TClassGeneratedArgs (and, for this purpose, other data types in the script), you can use the embedded debugger. In the *Script* tab, click *Debug* and, in the debugger, select the *View* ➤ *Library* menu. You will be able to explore the whole class tree the scripting engine uses.

For TAgent, we need to declare that the class inherits from TBase and then remove the ID (primary key) field, property, and attribute.

1. In the same procedure in the script, add the following code. This will make TAgent an ancestor of TBase.

```
procedure OnClassGenerated(Args: TClassGeneratedArgs);
begin
  if Args.CodeType.Name = 'TAgent' then
  begin
    // Add the Base class
    Args.CodeType.BaseType:=TCodeTypeReference.Create
    ('TBase');
  end;
  ...
end;
```

Next, we remove the FID field, the ID property, and the Id attribute from the class. The process is the same for all three things and, therefore, I will just show the code.

```
procedure OnClassGenerated(Args: TClassGeneratedArgs);
var
  field: TCodeTypeMember;
  attr: TCodeAttributeDeclaration;
  i: integer;
begin
  if Args.CodeType.Name = 'TAgent' then
  begin

    ...

    // Remove the ID Field
    for i:=Args.CodeType.Members.Count - 1 downto 0 do
    begin
```

```
      field:=Args.CodeType.Members.Items[i];
      if field.Name='FID' then
      begin
        Args.CodeType.Members.Delete(i);
        break;
      end;
    end;

    // Remove the ID property
    for i:=Args.CodeType.Members.Count - 1 downto 0  do
    begin
      field:=Args.CodeType.Members.Items[i];
      if field.Name='ID' then
      begin
        Args.CodeType.Members.Delete(i);
        break;
      end;
    end;

    // Remove the ID Attribute
    for i:=Args.CodeType.CustomAttributes.Count – 1
    downto 0 do
    begin
      attr:=Args.CodeType.CustomAttributes.Items[i];
      if attr.Name='Id' then
      begin
        Args.CodeType.CustomAttributes.Delete(i);
        break;
      end;
    end;
  end;
  ...
end;
```

Note that I iterate through the `Members` object list twice because removing an item affects the list itself, and I am not sure how sophisticated the script interpreter is. Additionally, the interpreter does not understand the `for..in` loop notation. You can find the script in the code files (`DataModelerScript.pas`).

Summary

In this chapter, we look at another tool that accompanies Aurelius and can assist developers. TMS Data Modeler provides a way to implement model- and database-first approaches, and it adds value by automating the entity units Aurelius consumes. At the same time, the tool offers a flexible way to customize the final units.

Index

© John Kouraklis 2019
J. Kouraklis, *Introducing Delphi ORM*, https://doi.org/10.1007/978-1-4842-5013-6

D

E

F, G, H

I, J, K